HOTSPOTS
TUNISIA

KU-384-137

Written by Conor Caffrey, updated by Sarah Thorowgood

Published by Thomas Cook Publishing
A division of Thomas Cook Tour Operations Limited.
Company Registration no. 1450464 England
The Thomas Cook Business Park, Unit 9, Coningsby Road,
Peterborough PE3 8SB, United Kingdom
Email: books@thomascook.com, Tel: + 44 (0) 1733 416477
www.thomascookpublishing.com

Produced by Cambridge Publishing Management Limited
Burr Elm Court, Main Street, Caldecote CB23 7NU

ISBN: 978-1-84157- 861-3

First edition © 2006 Thomas Cook Publishing
This second edition © 2008
Text © Thomas Cook Publishing,
Maps © Thomas Cook Publishing/PCGraphics (UK) Limited

Series Editor: Karen Fitzpatrick
Production/DTP: Steven Collins

Printed and bound in Spain by Graficas Cems, Navarra, Spain

Cover photography © Reinhard Schmid

CONTENTS

INTRODUCTION 5
Getting to know Tunisia 8
The best of Tunisia 10
Symbols key 12

RESORTS 13
Hammamet 15
Port el Kantaoui 21
Sousse...25
Monastir...31
Djerba 37

EXCURSIONS 43
Tunis..45
Carthage...54
Sidi Bou Said 58
Dougga 63
Nabeul...66
Kairouan...70
El Djem...74
Mahdia...76
Matmata 78
Desert safari 82

LIFESTYLE 89
Food & drink....................................90
Menu decoder 94
Shopping 96
Children..98
Sports & activities 100
Festivals & events 102

PRACTICAL INFORMATION 105
Accommodation.............................106
Preparing to go 108
During your stay 114

INDEX 125

MAPS
Tunisia 6
Hammamet 14
Port el Kantaoui 20
Sousse 24
Monastir 30
Djerba 36
Tunis..44

WHAT'S IN YOUR GUIDEBOOK?

Independent authors Impartial, up-to-date information from our travel experts who meticulously source local knowledge.

Experience Thomas Cook's 165 years in the travel industry and guidebook publishing enriches every word with expertise you can trust.

Travel know-how Contributions by thousands of staff around the globe, each one living and breathing travel.

Editors Travel-publishing professionals, pulling everything together to craft a perfect blend of words, pictures, maps and design.

You, the traveller We deliver a practical, no-nonsense approach to information, geared to how you really use it.

● *Colourful Tunisian doorway*

INTRODUCTION
Getting to know Tunisia

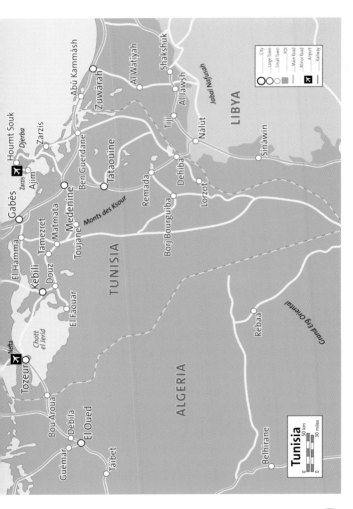

Getting to know Tunisia

Tunisia is one of the smallest countries on the African continent. Close to Europe, it is a fascinating mix of Mediterranean and Arabic cultural influences. With idyllic, unspoilt rocky coastline, sweeping sandy beaches, lush green vineyards and citrus groves to the north, and the harsh, desolate Sahara Desert to the south, Tunisia is an ideal holiday destination for those who want to experience a taste of the exotic without losing the comforts of a typical family holiday in the sun.

THE PEOPLE
Tourism is Tunisia's main industry and the Tunisians are genuinely warm and friendly to visitors. If you are lucky enough to experience the famed Arab hospitality, you will enjoy a holiday that you will never forget. Tunisians have the reputation of being the most liberal minded of the Islamic nations. Most of the people are a mix of Arab and Berber (the desert people) descent.

HISTORY
Tunisia has a chequered history and, although essentially a new country, people have been living there from early times. Not much is known about these early people, but it is likely that they were the ancestors of the modern-day Berbers who still live in the desert. It was not until the Phoenician traders (from Lebanon) arrived in around the 8th century BC and founded the trading posts, including Sousse and Carthage (just north of Tunis), that Tunisia and the Punic identity began to form. At one stage, Carthage was the capital of the great Phoenician empire, but after three wars with the Romans, Carthage was destroyed in 146 BC and the Romans took over. Julius Caesar rebuilt Carthage and it became the capital of the Roman Empire in Africa for 600 years. The German barbarians, the Vandals, followed by the Byzantines, then took over the area for a little time until the Arabs arrived at the end of the 7th century. The Arabs made Tunis their capital because they felt it was better protected than Carthage. They introduced Islam and the social structure

and culture that exist in the country today. The Arabs ruled Tunisia until the country became a French protectorate in 1881, and the French influence is still visible. During the German occupation of Tunisia in World War II, the independence movement began to grow through the actions of Habib Bourguiba, a lawyer educated in France, and his Néo-Destour movement. In 1957, he became the country's first president when Tunisia finally gained independence. Bourguiba's successor, President Ben Ali, who has just celebrated 20 years in power, rules today over a peaceful and stable Islamic country.

⬥ Ruins at Dougga (see page 63)

THE BEST OF TUNISIA

TOP 10 ATTRACTIONS

- **Tunisian beaches** are world famous. Along the entire stretch of the east coast there are seemingly endless white sandy beaches looking onto the beautiful azure Mediterranean Sea.

- **Watersports** The resorts of **Hammamet** (see page 15) and **Monastir** (see page 31) offer holidaymakers all kinds of watersports and other activities.

- **Desert Safari** No visit to Tunisia would be complete without a trip to the Sahara Desert. Witnessing the way of life of the local people is something that you will never forget (see pages 82–8).

- **Medinas** The heart of Tunisian life is found in its medinas, the old Arabic walled cities that are the centre of all Tunisia's main towns. The best are in Tunis (see page 46), Sousse (see page 26) and Kairouan (see page 72).

- **Go shopping in the souks** to see the colourful carpets, mountains of toy camels and smell the waft of aromatic spices or exotic perfumes.

- **Dougga** in the northwest of the country, is the most impressive ancient Roman site outside Europe and has a spectacular hilltop location (see page 63).

- **Carthage** The ancient Tunisian capital (see page 54).

- **El Djem** The amphitheatre at El Djem should also not be missed (see page 75).

- **The mosques of Tunisia** are usually spectacular in their simplicity and geometric symmetry. Kairouan's Grand Mosque is the most famous Islamic building in North Africa (see pages 71–2).

- **Tunisian architecture** The fortified Ibadite architecture on Djerba is markedly different to that of the mainland. Fadhloun Mosque outside Midoun (see page 41) is a good example of these fortified religious centres.

◆ *Medenine*

SYMBOLS KEY
The following symbols are used throughout this book:

ⓐ address **ⓣ** telephone **ⓦ** website address **ⓔ** email
ⓛ opening times **ⓘ** important

The following symbols are used on the maps:

i information office		○	city
✉ post office		○	large town
▣ shopping		○	small town
✈ airport		▪	POI (point of interest)
✚ hospital		═	motorway
⬛ police station		—	main road
▥ bus station		—	minor road
✝ church			

➊ numbers denote featured cafés, restaurants & evening venues

RESTAURANT CATEGORIES
Restaurants in this guide are graded by approximate price as follows:

£ = under 5 dinars   ££ = 5–15 dinars   £££ = over 15 dinars

◐ *The beach at Hammamet*

RESORTS
Places under the sun

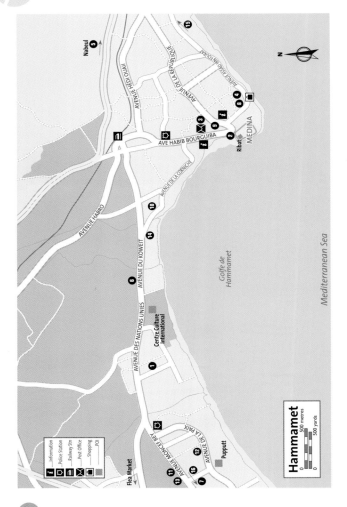

Hammamet

0   500 metres
0   500 yards

Nabeul

Mediterranean Sea

Golfe de
Hammamet

MEDINA

Ribat

AVE HABIB BOURGUIBA

AVENUE DE LA RÉPUBLIQUE

AVENUE HEDI OUAII

AVENU TASSO IBN FOURAT

AVENUE DE LA CORNICHE

AVENUE DU KOWEIT

AVENUE HABRO

AVENUE DES NATIONS UNIES

Centre Culture
International

AVENUE DE LA PAIX

AVENUE MONCEF BEY

Puptutt

Flea Market

Information
Police Station
Railway Stn
Post Office
Shopping
POI

Hammamet

This major resort town at the base of the Cap Bon peninsula is one of the most popular tourist destinations in Tunisia. In the 1920s, Hammamet was just a small fishing village with a thriving business exporting lemons, grown in the surrounding area, to America, but after a Romanian millionaire built a villa here the tourist industry took off. For a while, Hammamet was a cultural magnet for those who could afford a bohemian lifestyle that was exotic and exclusive. Many famous artists and writers, Paul Klee and André Gide among them, came to stay in Hammamet. But that bohemian exclusivity has all gone and now Hammamet is the biggest resort in Tunisia, with more tourist hotel beds than any other place in the country.

Although the visitors flock here in their droves during the high season, some of the original ambience of the town has been retained through sensible planning by the locals. None of the modern buildings is over a certain height, so they do not destroy the character of some of the original architecture.

As with many towns in the country, The Tunisians have conserved the historical centre by ensuring that facilities developed for tourists tend to be a little way outside the town centre. Hammamet has two 'zones touristiques'. There is a long strip of hotels to the northeast and Hammamet Yasmine, a new development opened in 2000 by President Ben Ali. The beaches around the town are excellent and stretch almost uninterrupted all the way north to Nabeul.

THINGS TO SEE & DO

Centre Culture International (International Cultural Centre)
The International Cultural Centre occupies a 9 ha (22 acre) site, which features the elegant, white art deco villa of the Romanian millionaire George Sebastian – a good place for a coffee. There are botanic gardens and a mock Greek theatre that is used to stage events during the annual summer art festival. Both Antony Eden and Rommel stayed here during

⬥ *The Ribat at Hammamet*

the war, and Rommel made it his Tunisian headquarters. Take a taxi from the centre of Hammamet or your hotel.

ⓐ Avenue des Nations Unies ⓣ 72 280 410 ⓛ 08.30–18.00 (summer); 09.30–17.00 (winter) ⓘ Admission charge

Flea Market

There is a flea market held on Thursdays in Hammamet outside the town centre, just to the north of the town. It is wise to go early because there is no shade and it gets very hot in the middle of the day.

The medina

The old walled medina was originally built in the 13th century as an extension of the Ribat that was still completely fortified by walls, and then rebuilt in the 15th century. It is quite a small medina, but if you wander away from the souvenir sellers' shops, you will find yourself almost alone among the whitewashed houses and traditional blue doors. Beyond some of the doors are pretty courtyards; others, brightly painted, will lead you to Turkish baths (hammams) (see page 61). If you are feeling extravagant, head for the lovely shop *Fella* which sells beautifully made Tunisian clothes and fabrics. ❶ 72 280 426

Pupputt

An archaeological site that was once an important Roman town in the 2nd–6th centuries AD, it is only really for serious ruin hunters although there are some good mosaics and a *souterrain* (underground passage). ⓐ In the Zone Touristique near the Hotel Temfouz ⏰ 09.00–13.00 & 14.00–17.00 ❶ Admission charge

The Ribat

First built in the 12th century, the Ribat has been rebuilt and restored many times. The French Foreign Legion was once garrisoned here. There are great views from the ramparts. Stop for a coffee at the small café Sidi Bou Hadid, which is a great place to relax. ⏰ 08.00–20.00 (summer); 08.00–18.00 (winter) ❶ Admission charge

TAKING A BREAK

La Bamba £ ❶ A friendly and inexpensive pizzeria that serves a variety of European snacks but which has an authentic Tunisian feel to it. ⓐ 25 Avenue Dag Hammarskjoeld ❶ 22 627 030

Café Achiri £ ❷ On the edge of the medina, this is the perfect place to watch Hammamet buzz while you relax with a mint tea or *shisha*. ⓐ On the northeast corner of the medina

🔺 *Seafront café, Hammamet*

Magasin Général £ ❸ Handy for beach food. ⓐ Avenue de la République ① 72 280 903 🕐 08.00–12.30 & 15.00–19.00 Tues–Sat, 08.00–13.30 Sun

Belle Vue ££ ❹ Good view, as the name implies. Selection of food from *briks* (deep-fried pastry parcels) and fish to pizzas. ⓐ Commercial Centre, off Avenue Habib Bourguiba ① 72 280 825

Chez Achour ££ ❺ One of the best restaurants in town. Excellent seafood, especially fish couscous, and traditional lamb recipes. ⓐ Rue Ali Belhaouane ① 72 280 140 🕐 12.00–24.00

Sidi Slim ££ ❻ Smart restaurant, a cut above average but still not too expensive. Specialities include fish baked in sea salt and camel steaks done the Berber way. ⓐ Avenue du Koweit 156 ① 72 279 124

Pomo Doro £££ ❼ An upmarket restaurant serving Italian as well as some traditional Tunisian dishes. ⓐ Port de Plaisance, Yasmine Hammamet ① 72 240 757

Les Trois Moutons £££ ❽ A gourmet restaurant serving Tunisian and international cuisine with fish and seafood as its specialities. ❹ Commercial Centre, off Avenue Habib Bourguiba ❶ 72 280 981 ❺ 11.30–14.30 & 18.00–23.00 ❗ Booking essential

AFTER DARK

Bars & clubs

Brauhaus ❾ A German-style pub, this is the best place for Bavarian home-brews. Restaurant upstairs serves cheap and cheerful fare. ❹ Opposite the medina in the centre of town

The British Pub ❿ The original and the first in Tunisia. It's still a popular hang-out holding its own among many similar British-themed drinking holes. ❹ Rue Dogga ❺ 11.00–late

Calypso ⓫ Open-air club. Over 18s. ❹ Avenue Moncef Bey ❶ 72 226 803 ❺ 10.00–late

Manhattan Club ⓬ A club, restaurant and piano bar all in one, with a lavish interior. ❹ Avenue de la Paix ❶ 72 226 226

La Pacha ⓭ Well-known club which plays host to international DJs. ❹ Avenue Moncef Bey ❶ 72 226 324

Sinbad Hotel Bar ⓮ Offers traditional English breakfast and bacon butties (an unusual delicacy in these parts because Muslims do not eat pork). Disco bar/karaoke in the evening. ❹ Near the Hotel Bel Air in the Zone Touristique ❶ 72 280 122 ❺ 11.00 until late (summer)

Casinos

There are two casinos in Hammamet:

Grand Casino de Hammamet ⓯ ❹ Hotel Sol, Azur Beach ❶ 72 261 777

Grand Casino Yasmine ⓰ ❹ Hammamet Sud ❶ 72 240 777

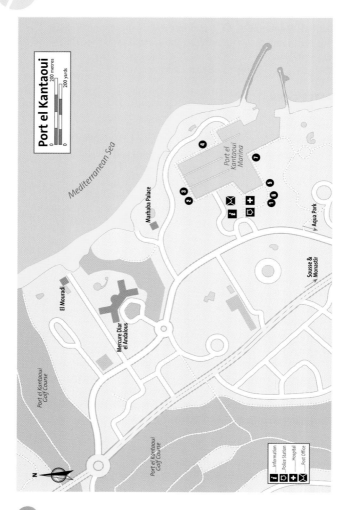

Port el Kantaoui

Port el Kantaoui

This is a purpose-built holiday resort, with a tasteful placement of restaurants and cafés around a marina frequented by the Mediterranean yacht set. The whitewashed hotels with their sculpted gardens and swimming pools give this resort the appearance of Mediterranean Spain, the south of France or even Greece.

Port el Kantaoui was built in the 1970s and is a good base from which to visit many of Tunisia's sights. The pleasant marina, which is surrounded by restaurants, cafés and souvenir shops, is a hub of activity. There is not much to see from a sightseeing perspective (though Sousse is not far away), but Port el Kantaoui is the perfect place to relax over a meal, do some shopping, play a round of golf or just while away the hours over an early-evening drink.

TAKING A BREAK

The following cafés and restaurants are in the marina. Prices at these establishments are all very competitive and really good value. For after-dark nightlife, you will end up at a disco in one of the central hotels – there's not much else.

Café Maure £ ❶ Great place to relax with a hookah pipe and one of the many different types of tea on offer. Choose from tea infused with milk, iced tea, tea with pine nuts, mint tea or tea with almonds. ⓐ Place de la Marina ❶ 73 348 799

La Roseraie £ ❷ Thirst-quenching fruit juices and tasty crêpes. Great view of the marina. ⓐ Place de la Marina

La Spada £ ❸ Excellent lunch option where great tuna sandwiches and pizzas are served. If you cannot decide whether to have a chicken or beef burger, this is the place for you – the house speciality Kantaoui burger contains both! ⓐ Place de la Marina

SHOPPING

You will find most of the best shops clustered around the picturesque marina, but nearby Sousse has a much better selection of handicrafts, especially leather.

Magasin Général Supermarket where you can purchase some goodies for a picnic on the beach.

Marina shop For leather belts and bags.

Sam Shop Olive-wood carvings and traditional dolls.

Select Shop Birdcages Provides an interesting piece of luggage to try to get home safely.

Tapis Scheherezade Excellent for leather goods.

🔺 *Gateway at Port El Kantaoui*

⬥ *The marina at Port El Kantaoui*

La Daurade ££ ❹ Specialises in fish dishes and *mezze* (mixed plate of dishes). You may need to book in high season. ⓐ Place de la Marina ⓣ 73 348 893 ⓛ Closed Mon

Les Emirs ££ ❺ Tunisian food and fish. Good place to try some lamb or share a *mezze*. ⓐ Place de la Marina ⓣ 73 348 700 ⓦ www.emiracity.com

Restaurant L'Escale ££ ❻ A smaller restaurant which serves the usual mix of French and Tunisian fare in pleasant terrace surroundings, set back from the marina a little way. ⓐ Place de la Marina

La Méditerranée £££ ❼ The best restaurant in Kantaoui, and the couscous is probably the best in the country (you will need to order this in advance). You definitely need to book even though it seats 250 people. English menu. ⓐ Place de la Marina ⓣ 73 348 788 ⓛ Closed Tues

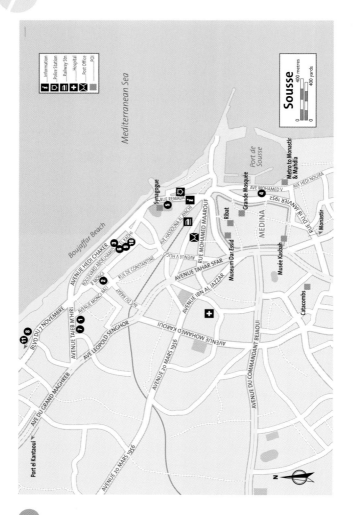

Sousse

With a population of about 170,000, the bustling city of Sousse is the third-largest city in Tunisia and a popular tourist resort as well as being a large industrial working port. Of all the resort towns this is the one where you are most likely to get a glimpse of local life, especially in the maze of the medina. Sousse was a major port in the time of the Phoenicians and used to be called Hadrumete. The natural harbour also attracted the Romans and the present city lies on the site of the Roman city of Hadrumetum. It was badly damaged during World War II but most of the town was rebuilt. The city centre is Place Farhat Hached on the edge of the main entrance to the medina and all roads lead into this square. Even the Tunis train passes through the middle of the street. Sousse has possibly the most impressive of town beaches in Tunisia, with the sandy Boujaffar beach only a short walk from the centre of the city.

THINGS TO SEE & DO

Catacombs

This series of underground early Christian burial tunnels dating from the 2nd–4th centuries AD is truly amazing and contrasts starkly with the busy centre of Sousse. Not for the claustrophobic, and far too dark for a camera, the caves offer little to see, but you can feel the eerie atmosphere. Unfortunately, there is only a small section open.

ⓐ Rue Abouel Hamad el-Ghazali – get a taxi from central Sousse, a distance of about 2 km (1¼ miles) 🕒 09.00–12.00 & 14.00–18.00 (winter); 08.00–12.00 & 15.00–19.00 (summer), closed Fri & Sat
❶ Admission charge

Grande Mosquée (Great Mosque)

Non-Muslims are only allowed into the courtyard of this mosque, which has a fortress-like appearance. You will have to rent a *jellaba* (hooded cotton cloak) to enter if you are wearing shorts or a short skirt.

ⓐ Rue el Aghlaba 🕒 08.00–14.00 Sat–Thur ❶ Admission charge

● *The beach at Sousse*

Medina

Sousse medina is a great place to get lost. It really has a lived-in feel and the old 9th-century walls are almost intact, except for a small area that was destroyed by Allied bombing during the war. Souk es Ribba is the main commercial thoroughfare of the medina. Be careful when you wander through the food market areas because butchers display items that you may not want to see before you eat. The **Museum Dar Essid** on the northwestern edge of the medina is a wonderful glimpse into the world of 19th-century Tunisian opulence.

Musée Kasbah (Sousse Archaeological Museum)

This museum is housed in a kasbah (old fort) spectacularly located on the top of the hill above the old medina to the southwest of the city centre. It is one of the best places to escape from the afternoon sun for a while, with large, cool rooms and incredible Roman mosaics – look out for those depicting Neptune and gladiators. Ten-minute walk up the hill from the entrance to the medina.

ⓐ Avenue du Maréchal Tito 🕒 0800–12.00 & 16.00–19.00 (summer); 09.30–12.00 & 14.00–18.00 (winter), closed Mon ❶ Admission charge

Ribat

This is the oldest monument in the city, dating from the 8th century BC. To get the best view over the city and the port, climb up to the top of the watchtower. Do not forget your camera.

🕒 08.00–19.00 (summer); 08.00–17.30 (winter) ❶ Admission charge

TAKING A BREAK

Bonaparte £ ❶ Good value for European-style food. Steak and chips, lasagne, pasta, fish and pizza. Child-friendly with 50 per cent off the bill for their meals. ⓐ Avenue Taieb M'hiri ❶ 73 225 342

Tip-Top £ ❷ One of the oldest restaurants in Sousse, this is an inexpensive and popular place that does great fish dishes and pizzas. ⓐ 73 Route de la Corniche ❶ 73 226 158 🕒 11.30–01.00

Forum Grill ££ ❸ Good fish cooked in rock salt. English menu. ⓐ Avenue Hedi Chaker ❶ 73 228 399

SOUSSE SHOPPING

There is a large market on Sundays in Sousse south of the centre of town. It is a lot less touristy than other souks you may visit and well worth a look if you are in town on the day. Hammam Sousse, a suburb about 5 km (3 miles) north of Sousse proper, also has more local markets on Friday night and Saturday morning. As well as food, you will find good-quality leather goods.

● *Puppet representing the popular hero Antar*

Le Lido ££ ❹ Cool during the middle of the day, with an old-fashioned wooden interior. Good for fish – try the grilled *dorado* (sea bream).
ⓐ Avenue Mohamed V, opposite the fishing boats in the port
ⓣ 73 225 329 ⓛ 11.00–14.30 & 17.30–23.00

La Marmite ££ ❺ Not named after something you either love or hate but after a type of Tunisian cooking pot, this place does good *mezze* and fish dishes. ⓐ 15 Rue Remada ⓣ 73 226 728

Una Storia della Vita £££ ❻ An up-market Italian restaurant serving an interesting mix of pastas and seafood. It also does some good stuffed pancakes. ❷ Boulevard du 7 Novembre ☎ 73 221 499

AFTER DARK

Bonaparte ❼ Popular pub and club, with karaoke. ❷ Avenue Taieb M'hiri ⏰ 20.30 till late ❶ Free entrance if you eat in the restaurant (see page 27). Happy hour seems to last all evening on certain nights.

Casino Caraibe ❽ For those who like a flutter in a Vegas-type casino. ❷ Opposite the Samara King on the Route Touristique. ☎ 73 211 777

Maracana ❾ The biggest nightclub (has three dance floors) in North Africa specialising in Techno music. ❷ Hotel Tej Marhaba, Boulevard du 7 Novembre

Rose and Crown ❿ A home away from home for those who really miss their local. A good atmosphere in the evenings. ❷ Hotel Tej Marhaba, Boulevard du 7 Novembre ☎ 73 229 800 (then ask for the Rose and Crown) ⏰ English breakfast served from 11.00 and pub grub at lunchtime.

Samara King Club ⓫ Most popular and professionally run club in town. ❷ Attached to the Samara King Hotel, Route Touristique ☎ 73 226 699 ⏰ 23.00–03.00

ANTAR

In many of the markets of Tunisia you will see some warrior-like wooden puppets for sale. These represent the great Arab hero Antar. He was both a warrior and a poet and he rose up from slavery to end up as a tribal chief. He is the popular hero of the epic *Sirat Antar* in which he is portrayed as a rich Bedouin chief who was brave, noble and kind.

Monastir

0 — 200 metres
0 — 200 yards

i ....Information
✈ ....Airport
🚉 ....Railway Stn
🚌 ....Bus Station
✚ ....Hospital
⛰ ....Post Office
🛍 ....Shopping
⬛ ....POI

N

Mediterranean Sea

Skanes Beach &
Habib Bourguiba
International

ROUTE DE LA FALAISE

Port de
Plaisance
Marina

Stadium

Mausolée
Bourguiba

The Ribat

Mosquée
Bourguiba

MEDINA

RUE DU MAROC

AVENUE HABIB BOURGUIBA

AVENUE FARHAT HACHAD

ROUTE DE LA FALAISE

Marché
Central

RUE IBN SINA

Port de
Pêche el
Ghadir

⬥ *The Ribat, Monastir*

interior and very good cuisine. Every first Sunday of the month there is a reasonably priced buffet and children under 12 years of age eat at half price. You may need to book because it does get busy during the summer months. ⓐ Marina ① 73 461 449

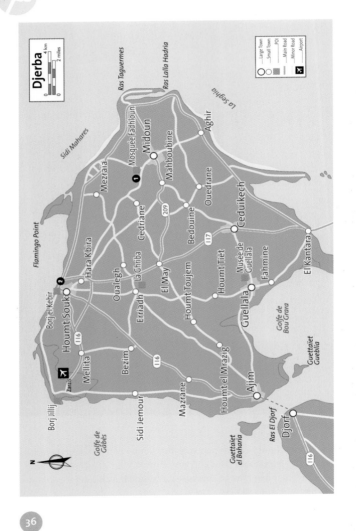

Djerba

Djerba is not actually a resort, but an island. Small, dry and sandy, the island, whose original Phoenician name, Meninx, means scarcity, has little rain and almost continuous sunshine throughout the year. It has become a sun-worshipper's paradise. Djerba has become increasingly popular as a holiday destination in spite of the fact that it still remains relatively underdeveloped.

Djerba has an ancient history and, according to legend, is the mythical land where Homer's Odysseus ate the 'fruit of forgetfulness' (the lotus). The traditional architecture of Djerba is distinctive and unique and betrays the unorthodox Ibadite identity of the island. The houses are white cubes each with a hemispherical dome on top.

The resort hotel area, the Zone Touristique, is on the east coast of the island. You can get to Djerba by catching the inexpensive car ferry from Djorf to Ajim. It is also possible to go via the Roman causeway, but this is a much longer route. Contact Tunisair for an internal flight to Djerba from the mainland. You will need to book in advance.

BEACHES

The best beaches are on the northeast part of the island. The beach at **Sidi Mahares** is the best and it stretches endlessly. Particular spots on this beach do get crowded at the height of the tourist season. It runs through the tourist centre with all the major resort hotels, and stretches from Flamingo Point, where you might spot some of these exotic pink birds, to the lighthouse at Ras Teguermes. **La Seghia Beach** on the east coast is also sandy and a good place to go kite surfing.

THINGS TO SEE & DO

La Ghriba

This ancient Jewish synagogue is one of the oldest places of Jewish worship in the world. 'La Ghriba' means 'the foreign woman' and the synagogue is built on a spot where a holy stone reputedly fell from heaven. It is a place of pilgrimage for Jews from all over the world. Most of the Djerban Jews emigrated to Israel when Tunisia attained independence, although there are still about one thousand living on the island. There is a special silver key to the synagogue and it is said that if the Jews ever leave the island, it will go straight back to heaven. One of the oldest Torahs (Jewish holy book) is kept in the synagogue. You must take off your shoes and cover your head when you go inside.

ⓐ 1 km (¾ mile) south of Erriadh 🕓 09.00–18.00 Sun–Fri ❶ Free admission

Guellala

This small, traditionally Berber village is the centre of the local pottery industry and is the place to come if you wish to buy any pottery. The clay

🔺 Potter's shop at Guellala

◯ *Borj el Kebir*

used is extracted from the hills above the town. The talented potters, who create some amazing and bizarre ceramic sculptures, will welcome you into their workshops. Cave Ali Berbere, south of the centre, is a particularly interesting and ancient pottery you can visit.

Musée de Guellala (Guellala Museum) Just east of Guellala, recently built – but based on original Ibadite designs that you will see all over the island – is this attractively designed museum. It is well worth a visit for a little more insight into traditional ways of life in Djerba and for the views over the south of the island (this, at only 50 m/55 yds, is the highest point of the island). The café outside is a pretty place to sit and take in the scene. Inside, waxworks model traditional wedding clothes – and you can even see some local depilation techniques!

ⓐ Guellala ⓣ 75 761 114 ⓛ 08.00–19.00 (summer); 08.00–17.00 (winter) ⓘ Admission charge

Houmt Souk

This is the 'capital' of the island and is a pleasant small town whose main street, Avenue Bourguiba, runs alongside the medina. Houmt Souk means 'market place'. The locals have preserved the distinctive architecture by ensuring that the holiday resort hotels were built a few kilometres out of the town to the west. There is a big market on Fridays.

Borj el Kebir This ancient 13th-century fort with its dramatic location looks out to sea over a harbour filled with small fishing boats. In the 16th century, it was the home of some of the infamous Barbary coast pirates, including Barbarossa and his prodigy Dragut Pacha.

There is a rather macabre monument to a massacre of Spanish forces by Dragut. He piled their skulls on top of one another to create a tower. You will be relieved to know that the skulls are gone and the site is now marked by a rather discreet obelisk. In front of the Borj el Kebir there is a market held every Tuesday and Thursday in the morning.

ⓛ 08.00–12.00 & 15.00–19.00 Sat–Thur (summer); 09.30–16.30 (winter) ⓘ Admission charge

Medina The central medina is not as authentic as it used to be, but there are some outdoor cafés and the whitewashed buildings are covered in colourful bougainvillea. The characteristic arched passageways at the entrance were traditionally where the most expensive goods were sold and this custom holds today. There is an incredible array of ceramics spread out on the pavement in front of the shops and you will probably spend a considerable amount of time weighing up your options before you decide on your favourite one to take home.

Mosquée Fadhloun (Fadhloun Mosque)

This disused but recently restored 14th-century mosque is on the road from Houmt Souk to Midoun, a few kilometres outside Midoun. If you are heading this way, stop here to see a classic example of the fortified Ibadite architecture for which the island is famous.

🕐 08.00–19.00 (summer); 08.00–17.00 (winter) ❶ Admission charge

⬥ *Pottery in the Medina, Houmt Souk*

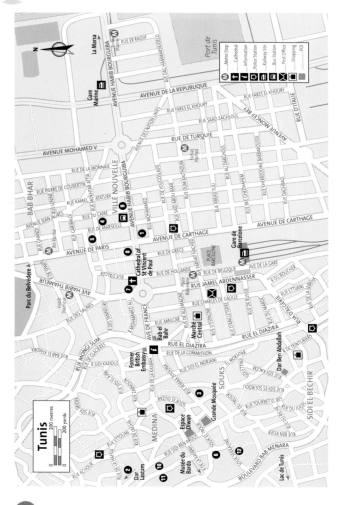

Tunis

Tunis is one of the largest Mediterranean ports and is a gateway to
Africa. It is an ancient city shaped over centuries and there have been
people living here since prehistory. The country's capital is nowadays a
sprawling metropolis in which about 20 per cent of the entire Tunisian
population lives.

The city centre is a strange mixture of the medieval Arabic Medina
and the colonial New Town, with the French influence evident in the
modern buildings and wide boulevards. You are in a modern Arabic city,
with new high-rise buildings, but which also has an ancient feel to it.
The city is flanked by the shallow **Lac de Tunis**, which you will see from
the plane if you fly into Tunis Airport. It was created artificially in the
9th century, when a canal was constructed to the sea, so it is salty, but it
does attract flamingos in the winter.

BEACHES

The chic suburb of **La Marsa** has one of the closest beaches to Tunis.
A 30-minute ride on the TGM (Tunis-Goulette-Marsa light rail – from the
Gare Marine at the end of Avenue Habib Bourguiba) will take you to the

⬤ *The beach at La Marsa*

end of the line and La Marsa. There is a sandy stretch of beach along a pleasant promenade.

THINGS TO SEE & DO

Dar Ben Abdallah (Museum of Popular Arts and Traditions)
This small but interesting museum was originally a palace in the centre of the medina. Built in the 18th century, it now provides a good escape from the hubbub outside, and shows how the local gentry lived in past times.
ⓐ Rue Sidi Kasem ⓒ 09.30–16.30 Mon–Sat, closed Sun
ⓘ Admission charge

Espace Diwan
You can buy books on Arab architecture and history, in a very picturesque setting (see the coloured glass mosaics on the ceiling).
ⓐ 9 Rue Sidi Benarous, La Medina ⓣ 71 572 398 ⓒ 11.00–19.00

Grande Mosquée (Great Mosque)
The Great Mosque has been the major focal point of the medina for over a thousand years. It dates from about AD 732 and has been enlarged and reconstructed many times since then. It is called the Zitouna (olive tree) mosque because it was founded by Hassan Ibn Nooman, who used to teach the Koran (the Muslim holy book) under an olive tree that used to be in this spot. You can enter the courtyard when it is open, but non-Muslims are not allowed in to see the interior of the mosque. The columns in the prayer hall were taken from Carthage. For one of the best views of the mosque, go into one of the nearby tourist supermarkets and ask to be allowed on to the roof.
ⓐ Medina ⓒ 08.00–12.00 Sat–Thur ⓘ Admission charge

Medina
The Tunis medina is the largest in the country and is classed by UNESCO as a World Heritage Site. A special local society, Association de

🔺 *Mosaic of Odysseus in the Bardo Museum*

Sauvegarde de la Médina, has its headquarters in the splendid **Dar Lastam** house which you can look round. The association was set up to ensure that the older buildings are conserved and maintained.

The major entrance to the old walled town is the old **Sea Gate (Bab el Bahr)**, also called Porte de France. It used to define the old city limits before the colonial French came to town. The elegant white building with the blue shutters right at the entrance to the medina was once the home of the British Embassy. Rue Jamaa ez Zitouna is one of the two main streets into the heart of the medina and it is lined with souvenir stalls. It ends at the entrance to the Grande Mosquée (Great Mosque), which is second only in age and importance to the Great Mosque in Kairouan (see page 71). Rue Zitouna is quite touristy and it is here that the hawkers will harass you the most. You will not get too many bargains when there are lots of tourists about, but there is a good choice of items on offer. The other main thoroughfare, Rue de la Kasbah, is equally bustling and sells more everyday items to locals.

◔ *The Great Mosque in the medina*

If you branch off into the narrow streets on either side of the Rue Jamaa ez Zitouna you will enter another world and catch a glimpse of what it was like to live in Tunis in medieval times. Here you will wander into special market areas (souks) that are each specific to one trade. One minute you will be in the perfumers' souk (Souk el Attarine) and the sweet smell of jasmine will fill your lungs, the next you will be in the wool souk (Souk de la Laine) and then in the Souk el Berka, now selling gold but at one time a slave market.

Although the boundaries of these traditional areas have become less defined than they used to be, you will still notice them. A map that is available at the Tourist Information office on Avenue Mohamed V shows three special marked routes you can follow. The map is useful, but you will still probably lose your way. Accept this and enjoy the atmosphere – you'll find your way out eventually!

Musée du Bardo (Bardo Museum)

The national museum is housed in a 19th-century Beylical (the Beys were Arab princes) palace west of the centre and it is the oldest museum in Africa. By far the best museum in Tunisia, it will help you to put the country's Roman and Punic ruins in perspective. The Roman mosaics covering both the walls and floors on the first and second floors are spectacular. Make sure you do not miss the huge, impressive floor mosaic covering both the walls and floors in the Sousse room. Look out for the mosaic of the poet Virgil flanked by two muses, and also one of Odysseus strapped to the mast of his ship as the three sirens try and lure him to his death with their sweet singing. There is some sculpture on the ground floor.

ⓐ Avenue du 2 Mars 1934 ⓣ 71 513 650 ⓛ 09.00–17.00 Tues–Sun (summer); 09.30–16.30 (winter); closed Mon and public holidays ⓘ Admission charge

Parc du Belvédère (Belvedere Park)

This patch of greenery is a good place to escape from the heat of the midday sun for a few hours if you are staying in the city centre for the

PERFUME

Tunis is famous for perfume and local perfumers used to have an international reputation for excellence. There is a special perfume market area in the medina (Souk el Attarine) to purchase local scents. Perfume-making is an ancient tradition in Tunis, but there are only a few remaining practising artisans. Even if you do not buy any perfume, it is worth stopping for a few moments at one of the shops to take in the smells and peer at the exotic bottles lined up on the shelves. Potions are made up differently for each individual, and the perfumer will blend together a whole series of essences and oils selected specifically for you. You can also buy one that is already made up, or some lavender, orange flower, jasmine or rosewater oil.

Tunisians often use perfumes to mark special occasions. At weddings, the guests are sometimes sprinkled with orange blossom oil, and Tunisians used to attach a special significance to where a small bouquet of jasmine was placed. A man placed it behind his right ear if he was available and behind his left if he was taken. A woman who accepted jasmine from a man signalled that she was interested in his attentions.

day. There is also a small and well-maintained zoo and a café in the middle of the lake.

❸ In the north of the city; take a no 5 bus and get off at Place Pasteur.

Ville Nouvelle (New Town)

This colonial part of Tunis centres on Avenue Habib Bourguiba, a wide, tree-lined boulevard lined with cafés and patisseries. The Catholic Cathedral of St Vincent de Paul, the art nouveau Old French Municipal Theatre, and the French and British embassies are most impressive. Rue de Marseille, which runs parallel with Avenue de Paris, has several restaurants and often stalls on the street selling some good luxury items such as soaps, linen and jewellery.

TAKING A BREAK

Café de Paris £ ❶ Good, clean café with air conditioning (interior can get a bit smoky). You can pay the premium and sit out on the street and watch the people stroll by. Coffee and pastries on offer. ⓐ Avenue Habib Bourguiba ❶ 71 240 583

Café Saf Saf £ ❷ This is the most famous café in town because it has a camel that draws water from a well, and some good coffee and a lively atmosphere. ⓐ Avenue 20 Mars ⓛ Only in summer.

Café ez-Zitouna £ ❸ The most Tunisian of the tiled cafés in the medina. Popular with those who work in the medina shops for relaxing over a hookah pipe and a cup of coffee after they have haggled with the tourists. It is a bit smoky, but at least worth a look for a glimpse of how the locals live. ⓐ Rue Jemaa Zitouna

⬥ *Avenue Habib Bourguiba*

SHOPPING

You need to haggle if you want to buy anything in the medina. If you prefer not to haggle, you can go to the **ONAT Shop** ⓐ Palmarium shopping centre, Avenue Habib Bourguiba ⓛ 09.00–17.30 Mon–Sat, 09.00–13.00 Sun

Or, if you want to know your money will go to a good cause, buy something at **Mains de Femmes**. This women's cooperative sells handmade goods produced by women in the poorest parts of Tunisia. ⓐ 47 Avenue Habib Bourguiba (upstairs in a small office space) ⓣ 71 330 789

La Mamma £ ❹ Serves mainly Italian cuisine but also Tunisian dishes. Can be busy but good value. ⓐ 11 Rue de Marseille ⓣ 71 240 109 ⓛ Closed July & Aug

Monte Cristo Café £ ❺ Authentic Tunisian fast-food place where a shish kebab will cost you less than a pound. Popular with a young local crowd, this is a good place for a bite to eat at lunchtime if you are very hungry! ⓐ Rue de Marseille, on the corner with Rue Moktar Jeld

M'rabet Café/Restaurant £ ❻ One of the most famous cafés in the medina because three holy men are buried here under the floor. An extremely peaceful place to escape from stressful haggling outside and to have a quiet mint tea. Good traditional food served in the restaurant upstairs. ⓐ Souk El Trouk in the medina ⓣ 71 263 681

Pâtisserie Ben Yaghlane £ ❼ One of the least expensive places for your early-morning cup of coffee and croissant. It is Tunisian in style and very clean – you stand in a room at the back to eat and drink. You will pay three times as much in the cafés with tables on the streets. If you do not want to linger, go here. ⓐ Avenue Habib Bourguiba at Place de l'Indépendance beside the cathedral ⓣ 71 753 767

Brasserie des 2 Avenues ££ ❽   A prime location for people-watching, but you do pay a little extra for the pleasure. This is a nice place to while away some time over a coffee. ❷ Avenue Habib Bourguiba, underneath the El Hana Hotel ❸ 71 331 144

Chez Nous ££ ❾   Serves typical French cuisine in a speak-easy type back room with a pre-war air to it. ❷ 5 Rue de Marseille, near the corner with Avenue Habib Bourguiba ❸ 71 254 043

Dar el-Jeld £££ ❿   A perfect example of traditional Tunisian hospitality, this is an exclusive restaurant in the medina, but not too expensive by European standards. The elegant yellow door at the entrance is worth a quick photograph. ❷ 5 Rue Dar el-Jeld, just off the Government Square ❸ 71 560 916 ❶ Booking essential

Dar el-Kheirat £££ ⓫   A new restaurant in the medina, this is a grand 17th-century palace restored to its former glory. Serves cocktails and traditional Tunisian dishes in various elegant rooms and patio courtyards. ❷ 19 Rue Dar el-Jeld ❸ 71 572 020 ⓦ www.darelkheirat.com

Essaraya £££ ⓬   Aristocratic and opulent palace converted into a restaurant with very good food. For those with a generous budget. ❷ In the medina, 6 Rue Ben Mahmoud ❸ 71 560 310 ❻ Closed Sun ❶ Booking required

HOOKAH PIPES

If you are a smoker you will probably want to try smoking a hookah pipe or *shisha* in one of the traditional Tunisian cafés. Hookahs do not contain any hashish, but cheap tobacco and molasses, which come in a range of flavours. The hookah pipes are for sale in most of the medinas and there are even specialist shops. If you do buy a hookah pipe, get someone to show you how it works before you try smoking it.

Carthage

This ancient city of Hannibal and Dido is now a modern, exclusive suburb of Tunis. It also happens to be the home of the Tunisian president's palace, as well as several embassies and some rather expensive-looking villas that drip with bougainvillea. Yet those seeking any remnants of its glorious pre-Roman past will find that the ancient site is not in very good shape. While this may be a little disappointing, with a little imagination you can quite easily picture yourself back to these times, when it was the most important city in the Western world, and appreciate the significance of this ancient site.

The great general Hannibal, who famously crossed the Alps on his elephants and went on to conquer Spain and invade Italy in 218 BC, was born here. And Dido, the legendary queen and tragic heroine of Virgil's epic poem *The Aeneid*, allegedly founded Carthage. According to legend, she fell in love with the wandering Aeneas who was fleeing the Trojan War, but their love was doomed because it was Aeneas's destiny to set off and found Rome. The gods were against Dido and she threw herself on a funeral pyre as Aeneas headed off in his ship.

Although this is a pretty good yarn, it is more likely that the Phoenicians from Lebanon, and not Dido, founded Carthage in 814 BC. They named it Qart Hadasht (New City), from which the name Carthage is derived. After a number of attempts, the Romans finally destroyed the city in 146 BC. Founded again in 44 BC, it lasted for 700 years under the Romans, the Vandals and the Byzantine Empire. The novelist Gustave Flaubert wrote a novel about ancient Carthage called *Salammbô*. Observant visitors will find that one of the Carthage metro stations is named after the main character in Flaubert's novel.

Visitors who want to see the ruins at Carthage can pay a single entrance fee for all of the sites – including the museum – which are all in different locations. ☎ 71 730 036 ● 08.30–17.30

◆ *The courtyard of the Roman villa Des Voilières*

◔ *Ruins at the Roman villas*

THINGS TO SEE & DO

Amphithéâtre (Amphitheatre)
Essentially a 2nd-century BC construction, this is the site of summer performances during the Carthage International Festival.

Musée National (Carthage Museum)
Good mosaics and impressive models here of the site as it was in ancient times.
ⓐ Beside the impressive old deconsecrated Cathedral of St Louis
ⓑ 08.00–19.00 (summer); 08.30–17.30 (winter)

The Roman villas
Although there is not much left of the villas, one has some excellent mosaics and it is worth a visit just to see these.

Thermes d'Antonin (The Antonine Baths)
The most visited of Carthage sites, the 2nd-century BC baths were the largest in ancient Rome, and even had places for dining. The rooms within the baths included steam rooms with fires underneath and cold rooms for bathers to cool off. Be warned – the nearby white villa is the president's palace. It is forbidden to photograph it, and armed guards will stop you.
ⓐ Carthage-Hannibal metro

Tophet
An ancient place where it is thought the Carthaginians sacrificed their first-born children to the gods.
ⓐ Salammbô metro

Sidi Bou Said

Sidi Bou Said is a picturesque small town perched on a hill high above the ocean, about 9.5 km (6 miles) west from the centre of Tunis. Its famed beauty is due to the blue doors of the traditional whitewashed houses. White is the colour of peace and blue is a colour associated with Islam. Flowering bougainvillea add a splash of Mediterranean colour to this town, which has tried valiantly to hang on to some of its authenticity in the face of coachloads of tour groups. It's a relaxing place to spend some time, and the half-hearted haggling of the local shopkeepers makes a pleasant change.

Your tour guide, if you have one, will probably take you up the main street, but to get a real flavour of the town, wander off into one of the little side streets and marvel at the architecture that could place this town anywhere on the Mediterranean coast. If you have the inclination and energy, you can climb to the lighthouse, from which there is a good view of the surrounding coastline, but there are plenty of other places for fantastic vistas. *Sidi* is the Arabic for 'saint' and Bou Said was a 13th-century Muslim holy man who settled in the village. There are

⬤ *Marina, Sidi Bou Said*

🔺 *Blue door, Sidi Bou Said*

some excellent art galleries and if you do have some extra money to spend on a local artist, then this is a good place to do it. Sidi Bou Said has always had a strong artistic community and it has attracted many great artists and writers, including Cervantes, Paul Klee and André Gide.

TAKING A BREAK

Some of Tunisia's best cafés are in Sidi Bou Said, and are ideal for a break from the midday heat.

Café des Nattes £ Climb the steps into this cool, traditionally decorated café and sit on the famous *nattes* (mats), or in an alcove on the balcony.
🄰 Right in the centre of town 🕐 71 749 661

◔ *The mosque*

Café du Port du Plaisance £ If you make the long, hot, strenuous hike down to the marina (not recommended in the heat of the day), this is a good place to sit and recharge your batteries. ⓐ Marina

Café Sidi Chabaane £ This café is a hive of activity all day and has good views of the marina and the coastline below. The short walk from the centre of town is well worth it and you can linger under a predictably blue umbrella with a pine nut tea or grab a crêpe at the new bar on the way in. ⓐ Rue Hedi Zarrouk

Restaurant Chargui £ Best value in the centre of town. Traditional dishes. Relax on the lovely terrace over lunch and enjoy the vista. ⓐ Rue Habib Thermer ⓣ 71 740 987

Au Bon Vieux Temps £££ Recommended restaurant with an elegant interior and a great view from the terrace. Food is excellent but pricey by Tunisian standards. The walls are lined with the pictures of local celebrities who have visited. ⓐ Rue Hedi Zarrouk ⓣ 71 744 733 ⓘ Booking essential

Dar Zarrouk £££ Beautifully appointed restaurant serving Tunisian and French cuisine in either the pretty courtyard or inside with stunning views out to sea. ⓐ Rue Hedi Zarrouk ⓣ 71 740 591

HAMMAMS

Traditional Turkish baths are very popular in Tunisia. They are inexpensive, probably the best way for you to keep clean when on holiday and a fascinating experience. There are hot rooms of varying temperatures and a rest room where you can relax. If you do not mind losing a few layers of skin, have a massage as well. You will feel fantastic afterwards. There are separate bathing times for men and women. One of the best baths in Sidi Bou Said is on Rue Ali Belhouane.

⬥ The Capitol, Dougga

Dougga

The ruins at Dougga (originally the Roman city of Thugga) are considered by many to be Tunisia's finest. The remains of the city, which was home for up to 10,000 people in its heyday, are in amazing condition, with the old roads through the city and many of the buildings still intact. You would think it had been abandoned only 50 years ago. Unfortunately, Dougga is probably a little too far from the southern resorts unless you stay overnight, but is well worth a day's excursion from the Hammamet area or Tunis. Rather than being turned into one big souvenir stall, Dougga's remote location has left the town relatively untouched by commercialism, apart from the obviously unofficial guides who do not speak any English.

You buy a combined ticket for all three ruins. ☎ 78 466 636 🕐 08.30–19.00 (summer); 08.30–17.30 (winter)

THINGS TO SEE & DO

Brothel (House of Trifolium)
The city's den of iniquity has survived and you can see the remains of a cashier's office, the prostitutes' cubicles, and a secret entrance for married men who wanted to come and go discreetly.

The Capitol
This is considered the finest Roman building in North Africa and it is one of the most beautiful, with its elegant golden stone Corinthinian columns shining brilliantly in the sunshine. It dates from the 2nd century BC and is dedicated to the Roman gods Jupiter, Juno and Minerva, whose statues used to be in three niches inside the building.

Latrines (Baths of the Cyclops)
There is one very well-preserved public lavatory at Dougga a little way down the hill. Here there are 12 latrines that face each other so the Romans could have a chat while doing their business. The baths, however, are no longer visible.

▲ *The Theatre, Dougga*

Theatre

This is the first building you see, because it is right by the entrance to Dougga. Although it is not as spectacular or as large as the one at El Djem, the theatre is well preserved and offers incredible views of the surrounding countryside. There are 19 rows of seats that could accommodate 3,500 people. It is the site for the classic theatre performances during the Dougga Festival in July.

The Tower (Mausoleum of Ateban)

Built at the foot of the hill, this Punic structure presents a mixture of architectural styles. It is one of the few remaining free-standing pre-Roman structures in Tunisia. Some of the fine original carvings that adorned this tower are now in the British Museum.

🕐 08.00–19.00 Tues–Sun (summer); 08.30–17.30 Tues–Sun (winter), closed Mon ❶ Admission charge

Nabeul

Nabeul is a small market town in the centre of an industrial area so it is more a trading point than a tourist resort. The main reason to visit the town is the Friday market, which takes over the whole town. Nabeul is the centre of pottery production in the country so wherever you buy pottery in Tunisia it is likely to have come from here.

You can buy practically any souvenir you want in the Friday market, which is also called the Camel Market (although the only camels you will see on sale now are stuffed toys). As well as the usual souvenirs and local pottery, there is a large vegetable and clothes market and a small area where they sell livestock, mainly sheep and goats.

The beach at Nabeul is a bit sad and deserted out of season and it is a good stroll from the centre. Things pick up during the peak season, when there are more tourists about, but it is a bit exposed and not as

⬤ *Nabeul is famous for its pottery*

attractive as the beaches at Hammamet. The tourist office is quite a way from the centre of town on Avenue Taïeb M'hiri. Outside the town there is a Zone Touristique with the resort hotels and this is where Nabeul's best beaches can be found.

SHOPPING IN NABEUL

The advantage of shopping at the Friday market in Nabeul is that you can buy all of your souvenirs in one spot. Coachloads of tourists come here from all over the north of Tunisia and this can both help and hinder you when you want to get a bargain. The sellers tend to be less likely to haggle with you (this does not mean they will not hassle you to buy something) and you are unlikely to get a great reduction in the asking price. On the other hand, because there is so much competition it can be a good place to buy because the sellers usually aim for a high volume of sales and a low margin of profit.

Coral

Although not particular to Nabeul, you will see a lot of coral jewellery for sale. Mediterranean coral is an endangered species – you should avoid buying coral jewellery since doing so hastens its extinction.

Grass mats

Another of Nabeul's specialities is the grass mats that you see sold all over the country – especially as individual portable prayer mats and in the prayer halls of mosques. You can see people making them in the workshops along the Rue des Nattiers. Some of them have very intricate designs and are real works of art, others are more for everyday use. Bear in mind if you are planning to buy one of these that it takes one person about a day to make about 1.5 sq m (16 sq ft) of mat.

Metalwork

The metalwork on sale is generally brasswork of low quality (so do not pay too much), but you can buy some pretty trays, coffee pots and teapots. Hawkers invariably start tapping away at a piece of an old tray

● *Buying a hookah at Nabeul's Camel Market*

or teapot when they see a tourist approaching, but they are unlikely to be actually making something in front of you.

Pottery

Nabeul is the national pottery centre and there is a vast array of pottery on display in the shops and in the Camel Market. From ancient Roman times, Nabeul has been exporting pottery to Europe. Most of the modern potters are heavily influenced by the lead glazing and styles of the potters of the Spanish province of Andalusia, who came here as refugees years ago. These styles are the most popular ones with the tourists, but you can also buy unglazed pottery still made using ancient Roman methods.

The island of Djerba is also famous for its pottery and a lot of the potters in Nabeul were originally Djerbans. They must have been attracted here by the good local clay for their craft. Just west of the town is a new potters' quarter where you can see things being made in front of you. This is the powerhouse of the Tunisian pottery industry and well worth a visit.

Stone carving

Dar Chaabane, a small town just north of Nabeul, is famous for its stone carvings as well as its pottery, and the limestone and sandstone adornments for doorways and lintels you see about the place are particularly attractive. You might want to purchase your house number with an Arabic motif, but remember that it may be heavy and difficult to carry home in your luggage.

TAKING A BREAK

Café Dar Essouk £ A beautifully appointed, chic and intimate place to retreat from the hubbub of the market place. Serves tea, coffee, *shisha* and pastries. ⓐ Avenue Farhat Hached ⓣ 98 534 345

Café Errachida ££ Best place for a mint tea with a little plate of delicious pastries. ⓐ On the corner of Avenues Bourguiba and Habib Thameur

Au Bon Kif £££ Good for fish. ⓐ On the corner of Avenues Marbella and Habib Thameur ⓣ 72 222 783

L'Olivier £££ Best restaurant in Nabeul, patronised by the local great and good, with a selection of Tunisian and French dishes. ⓐ Avenue Hedi Chaker ⓣ 72 286 613

Kairouan

This is the most holy of Tunisia's, and perhaps even North Africa's, Islamic cities. It is often referred to as the city of 50 mosques, and there are said to be at least that number in the medina alone. However, for non-Muslims there are only two mosques that you can visit without feeling intrusive (see pages 71 and 72). Commerce is important to Kairouan as well, though, and the city is the country's carpet-producing capital. This is the place to make a purchase if you want a carpet to take home.

There is one joint admission charge for all of the tourist attractions in Kairouan, so you only need to pay once. Hold on to your ticket.

⬤ Bassins aghlabides

THINGS TO SEE & DO

Bassins aghlabides (Aghlabite Basins)

These are three restored water reservoirs dating back to the Aglabite era (8th century AD) that have been in use until quite recently. You can look down on them from the roof of the tourist centre.

ⓐ Avenue de la République 🕐 09.00–12.00 & 15.00–19.00 (summer); 09.00–17.00 (winter) ❶ Admission charge

Grande Mosquée (Great Mosque)

There has been a mosque on this site since AD 670, but what you see today is a heavily restored building dating from the 9th–10th centuries AD. Built by the Arab general Uqba bin Nafi al-Fahri, the founder of Kairouan, the mosque is one of the finest examples of Islamic architecture in the world and it is the oldest Islamic site in North Africa. Tourists can enter the courtyard, but non-Muslims are not allowed to pass beyond the great cedar doors into the interior prayer hall.

🔺 *Detail of carpet for sale*

SHOPPING

You need to know what you are talking about when you choose a carpet. Although there are some quality carpets produced in Tunisia, even the expensive ones are unlikely to be heirlooms. But there is undoubtedly considerable choice as well as a lot of competition for trade in Kairouan and sellers employ several tactics to attract tourist trade. Do not believe the person who tells you he is a government-employed guide and leads you to a 'carpet museum'. Enter one of these shops and you will almost certainly emerge with a considerably lighter wallet. At the **Centre des Traditions et des Métiers d'Art de Kairouan** (just north of Hotel Barrouta in the medina) you will be able to see carpet making techniques demonstrated, buy a carpet at a fixed price, and arrange for it to be shipped back home after the payment of a small deposit (rest of payment and VAT due on delivery).

ⓐ Place des Martyrs ⓛ 07.30–14.00 Sat–Thur, 08.00–12.00 Fri (summer); 08.00–14.30 Sat–Thur, 08.00–12.00 Fri (winter) ❶ Admission charge

Medina

This ancient, walled city is a delight to wander round, although like all medinas of any size, a little labyrinthine. But do not worry about being lost – someone will always point you in the right direction if necessary. There are many stalls here where you can buy the usual souvenirs as well as some decent carpets, although you will need to be practised at haggling to get a bargain. In the middle of the medina you will find a 500-year-old well (ask for **Puits Barrouta**). It still draws water by camel (although mainly for tourists these days) from 20 m (65 ft) below ground.

Mosquée Sidi Sahbi (Sidi Sahbi Mosque)

A very holy mosque due to the fact that its founder, Abou Zammaa el Belaoui, was a companion of the Prophet. He used to carry three of the Prophet's beard hairs on his person. The other name for this mosque is the Mosque of the Barber. Non-Muslims are allowed into the interior courtyard of the mosque, but cannot see the saint's tomb. Founded in the 7th century, much of the building is actually 17th century.

ⓐ Ave Lama el Belaovi ⏱ 08.30–14.00 ❶ Admission charge

TAKING A BREAK

Sabra £ A small place serving good-value food. ⓐ Avenue de la République ❶ 77 235 095

Piccolo Mondo ££ Serves pizza and Tunisian food. ⓐ Avenue Ibn Jazzar (near Aghlabite Basins) ❶ 77 228 879

Roi de Couscous ££ As its name suggests, this is a good restaurant for couscous, and lamb. ⓐ Avenue 20 Mars

⬤ *The Great Mosque*

El Djem

The town of El Djem's one major attraction for tourists is the ruins of the Roman colosseum. As you approach, you can see the walls of the colosseum rising up above the low-lying buildings of El Djem. The colosseum is built on the site of the Roman city of Thysdrus, which was a wealthy town and much bigger than the small town that exists today. The town is surrounded by olive trees and the area provided olive oil for Rome. There were many luxurious villas in the vicinity, the remains of some of which you can see at the excellent museum. El Djem is also famous for its mosaics, which you can buy (although they can be heavy).

◆ *The Roman amphitheatre*

THINGS TO SEE & DO

Archaeological Museum

This museum is almost as much of a treat as the amphitheatre itself. As well as a mosaic collection to rival the Bardo Museum and some fine sculpture, all taken from the houses of ancient Thysdrus, you can wander round some fascinating excavations behind the museum and see more mosaics still in place on the floors of the houses. There is also the intriguing and meticulous reconstruction of a Roman villa known as the House of Africa.

ⓐ Sfax road ⏱ 07.00–19.00 (summer); 08.00–17.30 (winter)
❶ Admission charge

Roman amphitheatre (colosseum)

This is by far the most impressive Roman ruin you will see in Tunisia, unless you journey to Dougga. Gordian, the African proconsul to Rome, built the colosseum. He was quite a character, and, at the grand old age of 80, decided to rebel against the Roman Empire. When Gordian's attempted rebellion collapsed, he took his own life in the colosseum itself. It is only partially finished for this reason, but the architectural achievement is all the more impressive when you realise that the existing structure was originally clad in marble that had come all the way from Italy. As well as being incomplete because it was never finished, the amphitheatre's north wall has also been used as a quarry for other local construction since the fall of the Roman Empire. You can see where attempts were made in the late 20th century to reconstruct some of it in modern stone – a project that was halted when people realised that the authentic atmosphere of the site was in jeopardy.

⏱ 07.00–19.00 (summer); 08.00–17.30 (winter) ❶ Admission charge

International Symphony Festival

During the summer, an international symphony show is performed within the colosseum at night. The whole area is candle-lit, creating a charming and memorable atmosphere.

Mahdia

Mahdia is a small but expanding traditional fishing port, which remains relatively underdeveloped as a tourist resort. There is a relaxed pace to the town and it is a good place to wander through the traditional medina or among the fishing boats in the morning to see the fishermen fixing their nets. In the past Mahdia was an important fortress town for a strict splinter Islamic sect called the Fatimids, who tried to seize the seat of Islamic power from the family of the Prophet Mohammed and made Mahdia their capital. Most of the tourist hotels are located outside the town centre, which is a conservation area, in the Zone Touristique to the northwest of the town.

THINGS TO SEE & DO

Borj el Kebir (Big Tower)

This old fort was built by the Turks. Climb to the top of the tower for the best view of the harbour and fishing boats.

🕒 09.00–12.00 & 14.00–18.00 Tues–Sun (summer); 09.00–16.00 Tues–Sun (winter) ❶ Admission charge

🔺 *Fishing boats at Mahdia*

Covered market

Right beside the main harbour there is a small covered vegetable and fish market. The fish market on the right as you enter is crammed with the catch of the day, which you are likely to eat in one of the restaurants. Bunches of octopuses and prawns are plucked from large piles in trays and sold, but there are also some strange-looking, exotic fish that you will not recognise.

Grande Mosquée (Great Mosque)

A rather austere-looking building that was recently rebuilt on the site of the original mosque, which was crumbling into disrepair. Non-Muslims are not allowed entry.

ⓐ Place Khadi Noamine

Harbour

The pleasant harbour is filled with brightly painted fishing boats adorned with flags. In the late morning it will be filled with animated fishermen mending their nets. To the left along the coast you can see the old Fatimid fortifications and harbour.

Medina

This small, traditional medina is scenically located on a little peninsula jutting out to sea. There is a large sandstone gate that is more like a tunnel guarding the entrance. This is the Skifa el Kahla, which translates as 'dark hall'. On Fridays there is a local market held in the medina. Weaving is the local cottage industry; if you are interested you can visit one of the houses to see the traditional looms in action.

TAKING A BREAK

Café Sidi Salem £ The best-located café in town with an idyllic view out to sea. ⓐ On the corniche road by Borj el Kebir

Restaurant de la Medina ££ Unsurprisingly, fish is a speciality here
ⓐ Right by the fish market

Matmata

Matmata is an unusual place and you are unlikely to encounter a similar town anywhere in the world. To protect themselves from the harsh extremes of climate in the desert, the local Berber people built underground caves, or troglodyte homes. Each house is built around an open central courtyard, which you reach through a small door. Most of the doors have designs on them, painted in blue, often of the hand of Fatima, a fish or a camel. Many of these symbols are meant to ward off the evil eye and bring good luck to the home.

The underground living quarters are kept spotlessly clean, and have whitewashed walls and little cupboards and shelves carved into the rocks. In summer, the houses remain cool even in temperatures that soar above 49°C (120°F). In winter, night temperatures can fall to freezing, but the cave dwellers remain snug and warm. In the past, the underground homes were also useful for defence against raiders. The strange dwellings seem to be both medieval (there have been people living in them for over 700 years) and futuristic, carved into the lunar landscape of the desert.

Filmmakers have frequently exploited the strangeness and uniqueness of Matmata. Luke Skywalker of *Star Wars* fame lived here and uttered the immortal words 'I'm never gonna get out of here' just before he headed off to save the universe and duel with Darth Vader. In 1976, George Lucas's film crew rented the Hotel Sidi Dris in Matmata and the *Star Wars* epic began, starting with the shooting of the scenes on the Planet Tatooine.

Matmata went from being an obscure Saharan desert town to a major tourist destination. Over a million film buffs visited the site before the first *Star Wars* film was even launched. Many of the subsequent episodes of *Star Wars* were also filmed here, including the most recent, *Attack of the Clones*. *The English Patient* was also filmed in Matmata, although the actual events in Michael Ondaatje's book were set in Egypt.

A result of the tourist influx and subsequent modernisation of the town is that most villagers now live above ground and have all mod

◯ *Troglodyte home, Matmata*

◯ *The picturesque town of Toujane*

cons. Some of them charge people to enter their former homes, which are preserved as museums. There are even a couple of hotels that were formerly underground homes. These are fun places to stay if you want to remain overnight in Matmata (see page 106).

The many troglodyte homes that are still inhabited are hidden away from the tourist's eye in the rugged desert landscape that surrounds the town. You will need to head out on foot away from the modern houses above ground to see the ancient way of living. Some guided tours include a camel tour out into the surrounding desert.

Tamezret and Toujane

Tours that go to Matmata may go to some of the villages nearby. Tamezret, to the west of Matmata, is a small, traditional desert town on a hill. It is worth climbing the hill here for some wonderful views of the surrounding terrain.

The old town of Toujane to the southeast of Matmata is probably the most spectacularly located town in the whole region. It is situated on the side of a steep gorge and you get the best view of the gorge and the town from the road from Matmata. Nouvelle Toujane, also called Dekhila, is on the plains, and is a boring town in comparison.

Desert safari

The Sahara is the largest desert in the world. Over 9 million sq km (3¹/₂ million sq miles) stretches from the Atlantic Ocean and into Iraq at the far side of the Red Sea. From north to south it runs for about 1,600 km (1,000 miles) from the shores of the Mediterranean, which it touches in places, to the Sudan and the River Niger. The popular image of a desert is of endless, wind-sculpted sandy dunes, with no plants at all except for the odd oasis filled with palm trees. In reality, this is not the case – most desert terrain is dry, dull, flat and uninteresting, and only two per cent of the desert is fertile.

A trip out into the Sahara is an exotic adventure that you will always remember. If you take only one excursion while on holiday in Tunisia, it must be to the Grand Erg Oriental (an area of sandy desert is called an erg) or Great Sand Dune Desert of the Sahara. Most desert is quite disappointing terrain, with arid, flat, rocky ground and only the odd low-lying bush to break the monotony. However, when you see a camel train cross the pristine sandy dunes of the 'real' Sahara, all those romantic images you have of the desert come alive before your very eyes.

DRIVING IN THE DESERT

If you have hired a car and are driving in the desert, you need to be very careful. Although you may have the air conditioning on and feel quite cool, it is very hot outside. You need to make sure you carry at least 5 litres (9 pints) of water per person per day in the car. You should also ensure that the car is in good working order before you make the trip. Stick to the major roads if you are not in a four-wheel-drive vehicle because minor roads can be in very bad condition and turn into what the locals call *pistes*, which are not really roads at all, but bumpy tracks filled with rocks.

If you do happen to break down in the middle of nowhere, the cardinal rule is that you stay with your car, since it is much easier to spot someone beside a vehicle than if they have wandered off alone on a mission to find help. The desert is an unforgiving place, with very little

△ The oasis of Chbika

EXCURSIONS

water, and you can get into serious trouble if you do not take precautions and keep hydrated. If you are doing some off-road exploring in the desert in a four-wheel-drive vehicle, make sure you let someone know where you are going and how long you intend to be away – you are advised to go in convoy with another vehicle as well. Hiring an experienced guide to go with you and show you the way is a much more sensible option.

THINGS TO SEE & DO

Chbika and Tamaghza
These are spectacular villages – you can see a palmery and waterfalls in the heart of the desert (about 60 km/37 miles from Tozeur).

Chott El Jerid
The large, dry salt lakes (*chotts*) of southern Tunisia mark the northern border of the Sahara Desert. The Chott El Jerid is the largest one in the Sahara at 5,200 sq km (2,000 sq miles). Chemicals in the salt affect the colour, and in bright sunlight there are some stretches of red, blue and green. You can see mirages when you drive through the *chotts* that will make you think you are seeing a lake filled with water. However, this only happens after a period of heavy rainfall.

MIRAGES
Driving through the desert, particularly over one of the salt lakes, you are likely to see a mirage – or at least you will think you have seen one. Mirages are optical illusions created by different layers of hot air. You can photograph mirages but, like a rainbow, you will never reach one. The mirage you see depends a lot on your imagination. Some people will interpret the images reflected in what looks like a cool pool of water as an ancient nomadic caravan train, while others will only see those tourist landcruisers that are everywhere.

⬥ *A trip to the Sahara is a must*

Douz

This small town is the gateway to the Sahara and probably the best place to go for a camel ride. Right on the edge of the Grand Erg Oriental of the Sahara, it is a 20-minute walk out over the first dune and into the desert if you are staying in the Zone Touristique. Do this at sunrise or sunset, when the light on the dunes is particularly magical and it is not too hot. Better still, you can jump on one of the camels for hire and head off for a few hours into the great sandy desert beyond.

The best day to be in Douz is Thursday, when there is a traditional market early in the morning. It is still authentic but it does have a touristy section with souvenirs for sale. It is the same sort of stuff you find everywhere. Try to get there as early as you can, because the market is most active before the day really starts to heat up.

Although it is called a camel market, you are more likely to see goats and sheep for sale than camels. There may be a few camels hanging around, but they are unlikely to be for sale unless they are the

◆ The medina and city walls of Douz

🔺 *Danger: camels crossing*

toy kind, which come in a variety of sizes, some nearly as big as the real thing. There is also an interesting vegetable market area and it is here and in the livestock area that you will see some of the locals doing business.

Ong Ejjmal

This place gets its name (Neck of the Camel) from a bizarre rock formation. The first *Star Wars* film was shot here (see page 78), as were scenes from *The English Patient*.

Tozeur

This oasis town is exactly how you would imagine a desert oasis should be. It has 200 natural springs, which produce 60 million litres (13.2 million gallons) of water every day. There is a huge plantation of about 200,000 date palms and this is the best place to buy dates to take home. The dates from here are called the *deglat en nour*, or 'finger of light'. They are known to be the tastiest in Tunisia and are said to be the best of all 120 date varieties. The date industry is very important to Tozeur (second to tourism) and a few thousand tonnes are exported each year, especially to Europe around Christmas time.

⬤ *Dates drying in the sun*

A carriage ride through the palm trees is the best way to see the palmery. Every piece of the palm tree is recycled or used by the locals. They even make *lagmi* (a sweet palm wine) from the sap of the tree.

Tozeur marks the last outpost of the Roman Empire in North Africa and gets its name from its Latin name *Thusuros*. Look out for intricate designs on the traditional brickwork in the medina.

▶ *Harbours are an ideal place to enjoy the sunshine*

Food & drink

Tunisian food is tasty and exotic, but it can be quite spicy. The food served in hotels and restaurants in tourist resorts tends to cater for European visitors though. If you prefer hot and spicy food, you should head off and explore the restaurants the locals use, many of which are of excellent quality, and inexpensive too.

⬤ *Pine nut tea*

BREAKFAST

Many of the hotels offer breakfast buffets with half board which usually include eggs, cold meats, cereals, cheese and fruit. Alternatively, you can try a patisserie or café and join the locals for a café au lait and an almond croissant. You could be breakfasting in France.

LUNCH & SNACKS

You cannot beat a *cassecroûte* for lunch. This is a tuna salad baguette sandwich and it often comes loaded with *harissa*. You can ask for it to be mild, as it can be mouth burning. *Harissa* (see page 92) is a very spicy hot pepper sauce and is only for those with strong constitutions – taste a little first! There are also plenty of places for cheap pizza, burgers or excellent kebabs.

STARTERS

In most restaurants you will be presented with a basket of bread with *harissa* on the side and some local olives when you sit down for your meal. A typical starter would be the local speciality *brik* (deep-fried pastry parcel with tuna or meat, egg and vegetables – with just egg it is called *brik à l'oeuf*), a Tunisian salad (a diced salad with tomato and cucumber), *mechouia* (a cold, roasted vegetable salad with sweet peppers), or a fish *chorba* (an oily but tasty spicy soup). The deluxe version of *brik* is with seafood (*brik aux fruits de mer*). *Ojja*, a kind of scrambled eggs often served with cow's brains, is worth a try.

MAIN COURSES

The Tunisian national dish is couscous (like a savoury semolina), and at its best it is fluffy and light. On its own it is pretty bland, but complemented by lamb, chicken or fish and vegetables it is delicious. It can be cooked in many ways and you are unlikely to taste the same recipe in two different restaurants. There are plenty of other choices on restaurant menus and in the resorts you will get a wide variety of familiar dishes from fish, such as *daurade* (sea bream) or *loup de mer* (sea bass), cooked very simply, to steaks and pizzas. You can also get some really good seafood with lobster, squid, oysters, shrimps and prawns at resort restaurants.

SPICES

Tunisians use a lot of colourful spices in their cooking and you will see them for sale in the markets. The orange crocus stamens of saffron are particularly good value, so it is worthwhile making a purchase if you would like to flavour your rice or cook paellas when you get back home. *Harissa* is a Tunisian paste consisting of mint, salt, chilies, cumin, coriander, caraway seeds and garlic.

VEGETARIAN

Tunisians do not really cater for vegetarians yet, although some of the restaurants in major resorts have started to include vegetarian options on their menus. You can order couscous without meat, but may still get it in a meat broth in some places. If you are not vegan, you can get dishes containing just cheese and eggs (such as pizzas and omelettes). If you do not eat any dairy products, you are going to have problems and a very limited diet. Stick to Western-style restaurants.

DESSERTS

Tunisian desserts tend to be very sweet and are a series of honey-soaked, sugary pastries filled with dates and nuts. You can try some of the very good ice cream or a sorbet after a meal, if you do not have a sweet tooth. Diabetics should avoid the ultra-sweet foods.

DRINKING

Some restaurants do not serve alcohol, but in the resorts most do. *Celtia* is a locally brewed light lager that is palatable and cheap. Imported beers are more expensive. Tunisia produces some good red and white wines.

Hot drinks Coffee and tea drinking are part of the social fabric of Tunisia and the men can spend hours chatting over a black coffee or tea, while the women seem to do all of the work. Coffee is served in a range of

● *Makroudh – a type of local pastry*

ways. Black and strong, like a sweet espresso, is great for those needing a real caffeine injection. Some find this a little bit too sweet and a little gritty. Café au lait (coffee with milk, which is a bit like a latte) and cappuccino are very similar to what you would drink in a café in Europe. Tea is green with sprigs of mint in a glass or with pine nuts or almonds. Red tea is very stewed and is an acquired taste. Both are sweet. You are unlikely to get tea with milk, unless you are in one of the 'good' hotels. If you miss your cup of tea, you may have to wait until you get home, or you could describe English tea (black tea with milk) to your waiter.

Tunisian wine The wines of Tunisia are better than you might expect, considering it is a Muslim country and it is generally frowned upon to drink alcohol. Winemaking has been carried out on the Cap Bon peninsula since Phoenician times, so there is certainly no lack of knowledge of the subject especially once the French took control of the country. The Cap Bon peninsula has the ideal soil and dramatic conditions to make some very palatable, if not spectacular, reds, rosés and whites.

Menu decoder

Here are some of the authentic Tunisian dishes that you might encounter in cafés, restaurants or pastry shops.

Brik Deep-fried pastry parcel, with egg (*brik à l'oeuf*), tuna (*brik au thon*) or mixed seafood (*brik aux fruits de mer*) being the most common

Brochettes Small cubes of grilled lamb served on a skewer

Cassecroûte Baguette sandwich. Most often with tuna salad and lots of *harissa* (see below)

Chorba Spicy and oily soup with fish, meat or vegetables

Couscous Tunisian national dish. Semolina grains that are best fluffy and light, but rather bland on their own. Served in a myriad of ways with meat, fish or vegetables and a sauce

Harissa Hot, peppery red sauce usually served as a condiment in sandwiches or with bread in restaurants

Kamounia Casserole with strong cumin flavour that is made with chicken or meat

Kefta Meatballs usually served in a tomato sauce

Koucha Lamb casserole flavoured with rosemary and potatoes and sometimes cooked in an earthenware pot

Loup de mer Translates into English as 'wolf of the sea', but it is actually sea bass

Makroudh Sweet pastry stuffed with date paste

Mechoui Grilled meat dish

Merguez Spicy beef or lamb sausages

Mermez Lamb stew

Ojja Scrambled egg with hot tomato sauce and mixed with brains (*cervelle* – not to be confused with *crevette*, which is a type of prawn), meat or fish

Salade mechouia Chargrilled peppers and tomatoes served cold in a salad and topped with an egg, tuna,

BOAT TRIPS

From many of the resort towns you can take your children on a pirate ship excursion to see the dolphins in the Mediterranean Sea. In Port El Kantaoui there is even a yellow submarine for those who fancy a trip underneath the waves. Most resorts also run fishing trips too.

CAMELS & THE DESERT

Most children get a real kick out of seeing camels in the flesh for the first time. If they are brave enough, a ride on a camel is a real thrill. They can do this in the resorts, where there are usually camels that pass along the beach. The camels are usually docile, so you do not have to worry too much. If you do make a trip out to the desert oasis, riding a camel with your child in the dunes is a memory you will keep forever and one that will make for great pictures.

EATING OUT

The restaurants in the tourist areas as well as more local restaurants are always child friendly. The waiters will probably make a great fuss and have some fun with your children, even when they appear to be too busy to do so. Tunisians in general love children.

LAND TRAINS

In the major resorts, there are special trains that run along the road from the resort hotels to the beach and back. They are a fun way to travel if you are not in too much of a hurry. The drivers are very entertaining and usually put on a show for the children. In some resorts they have *tuk tuks* (small three-wheelers), and a ride in one of these can be just as much fun.

VISITING OLD RUINS

Deciding on whether to take your children to see some Roman ruins depends on their ages and interests. Some children find visiting ruins pretty boring, but others will have great fun running around pretending they are gladiators.

Sports & activities

There is plenty to do for those who like an activity-based holiday, with excellent water-based activities to keep you busy and entertained.

DESERT SAFARIS & CAMEL RIDING

You can go on organised Land Rover safaris that travel deep into the desert. Book these with travel agents before you go on holiday or at agents in any of the resorts in Tunisia. Ask your representative to recommend one if there is nothing organised already for your holiday. Riding on a camel is an experience you will never forget. You can do it at the beach or, even better, in the Sahara at Douz.

FOOTBALL

The Tunisians are football crazy and the country's national team qualified for the 2002 World Cup. The locals are always ready for an impromptu game of beach football, so if you are feeling energetic you can show off your ball skills and have some fun.

GOLF

Tunisia has become a really popular golfing destination – you may have to book a round before you leave for your holiday, especially in high season. Here are some of the best courses and the nearest resorts:

- **Djerba – Djerba Golf** 18-hole course (par 73), 9-hole course (par 31). 🕿 75 745 055 🖳 www.djerbagolf.com
- **Hammamet – Golf Yasmine** 18-hole course (par 72). 🕿 72 22 7001 🖳 www.golfyasmine.com
- **Monastir – Flamingo Golf Course** 18-hole course (par 72). 🕿 73 500 283 🖳 www.golfflamingo.com
  Palm Links Golf Course 18-hole course (par 72). 🕿 73 521 910 🖳 www.golf-palmlinks.com
- **Sousse/Port El Kantaoui – Golf el Kantaoui** 27-hole course (par 108). 🕿 73 348 756 🖳 www.kantaouigolfcourse.com.tn
- **Tunis – Golf de Carthage** 18-hole course (par 66). 🕿 71 765 700

⬥ *Beach parachuting*

SAILING & FISHING

You can hire sailing boats or go out on a catamaran for a day at
Port El Kantaoui, Monastir or Sidi Bou Said. You can also go out on a
relaxed sea-fishing trip or perhaps do some serious sports fishing.
You do not need a licence to fish in Tunisia. Wind- and kitesurfing are
also possible in many of the resorts and on Djerba.

SNORKELLING & SCUBA DIVING

Bring your snorkelling gear – the clear waters, good coral reefs and
diverse sea life make for excellent snorkelling. More serious divers can
do a course or go out with the professionals at Port El Kantaoui or
Monastir or Tabarka.

- **El Kantaoui Diving Centre** ⓐ At the Marina ⓣ 73 246 374
  ⓛ 09.00–17.00 Mon–Sat
- **Malidia, Cap Afrique** ⓐ By the harbour ⓣ 22 697 252
- **Monastir Dive Centre** ⓐ At the marina ⓣ 73 462 305
- **Odysea Diving School** ⓐ Hammamet ⓣ 72 280 588
  ⓦ www.odyseadiving.com

LIFESTYLE

Festivals & events

ART & CULTURAL FESTIVALS

There are a number of events held throughout the summer months that feature local theatre, music and dance. The major ones are at Dougga in July, Carthage in July–August and Hammamet (held at the International Cultural Centre) in August. Theatre performances are usually in French, so you will need to understand the language to follow the plays, but you will always be able to look at the spectacle of the show and make up your own words if you do not. There is a falconry festival held near Hammamet in El Haouaria each June. In addition, most resort hotels hold mock folk festivals at the weekends during the high season. These vary in quality and authenticity, but they can be fun or tacky depending on your point of view.

If you go out for a night of entertainment in one of Tunisia's resort hotels, you are guaranteed to hear traditional Malouf music. Malouf was

● *Mosaic at Sebastian's Villa, Hammamet (see page 15)*

● *Tunisians playing traditional Malouf music*

brought to North Africa by Muslim refugees escaping from persecution at the hands of Christians in Andalusia, Spain, in around the 15th century. It is thought to have originated in Iraq, but on its introduction to North Africa the Tunisians have made it their own national music. Malouf translates as 'that which is normal'. The music is usually played by a small band of musicians using lutes, violins, sitars and drums. It entrancingly combines song, Arabic poetry and musical interludes.

DESERT FESTIVALS

The Oasis festival is held at Tozeur in November. It features camel racing and Bedouin cultural events.

The larger Douz Festival of the Sahara is held in December/ November (depending on when Ramadan falls) and up to 50,000 Berbers, nomads and tourists congregate in the town for the festivities. It lasts for about a week and features camel racing, traditional weddings, greyhound racing, music, dancing and poetry contests.

FEAST OF ABRAHIM (AID EL KEBIR)

The second major Islamic feast is a low-key family affair and celebrates Abrahim's test of faith when he was asked by God to sacrifice his own son Ismael. It is like the Tunisian version of Christmas and family members travel from all over Tunisia to be with their families. Just as Christmas is a bad time for turkeys in our part of the world, it is a very bad time for sheep in Tunisia and other Muslim countries, because lamb is the major item on the menu.

RAMADAN

This is an important time for Muslims. It occurs at different times of year depending on the lunar calendar. It is a month-long festival of devotion and fasting during daylight hours. Many restaurants are closed and you might be forgiven for thinking that it would not really be a good time to visit Tunisia. In the evenings, however, the streets buzz with activity and all the restaurants and cafés are open late into the night. There is a tremendous atmosphere and impromptu musical performances and puppet shows in the streets and cafés. Ramadan ends with a big feast and public holiday on Aid el Fitr.

WEDDINGS

These are probably the only big festive occasions when Tunisians really let their hair down. Most weddings are held in the summer so family members can return from abroad. They are very public events and can last a whole week, with a procession, dancing, feasting and much merrymaking. If you are lucky enough to be invited to an authentic Tunisian wedding, you should jump at the chance. Staged weddings for the tourists are held in many resort towns, especially in Midoun on the island of Djerba.

● *The Marina at Sidi Bou Said seen from the town*

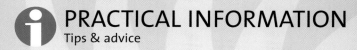

PRACTICAL INFORMATION
Tips & advice

Accommodation

All prices are for a double room per night for two people and breakfast only and are peak season (July–Aug).

£   under 180 dinars
££   180–270 dinars
£££ over 270 dinars

Hotel Marhala £ This is considered to be the best of the troglodyte hotels in Matmata (there are several). The underground rooms are very cosy, if basic, and they do not have bathrooms (you have to share bathroom facilities) – but then that's a small price to pay for an extraordinary experience. Book well in advance if you want to stay here.
ⓐ Matmata ⓣ 75 240 015

Hotel Médina £ An excellent budget choice right in the middle of it all in Sousse's teeming medina. The rooms are modern and clean with bathrooms. ⓐ 15 Rue Othman Osman, Sousse ⓣ 73 221 722

Hotel Yasmine £ A very reasonanly priced small pension with en-suite bathrooms and some rooms with balconies with sea views. Also has a small restaurant. ⓐ Route de la Falaise, Monastir ⓣ 73 501 546

Hasdrubal Thalassa Hotel & Spa ££ A typical resort hotel with four-star facilities including swimming pool. There are several similar places in Port El Kantaoui but this one is near the marina, which makes it very convenient. ⓐ Marina, Port El Kantaoui ⓣ 73 348 944

Marina Cap Monastir ££ A good mid-range choice in Monastir's pretty little marina. It's a basic resort-style hotel and not as upmarket as some, but has perhaps more character than some because of its position.
ⓐ Monastir Marina ⓣ 73 462 305

Résidence Romane ££ A relaxed, family-run property that enjoys an excellent central location. A great place to soak up the traditional Tunisian atmosphere that surrounds the nearby restaurants and cafés. ⓐ Rue Assad Ben Fourat 8050, Hammamet ⓣ 72 263 103

Abou Nawas Boujjaffar £££ A resort-style hotel with all the usual all-inclusive facilities, but more conveniently situated in the city centre and on the beach. Has a buzzing bar in the evenings due to its location. ⓐ Avenue Habib Bourguiba, Sousse ⓣ 73 226 030

Dar El Medina £££ A gorgeously decorated 19th-century palace converted into a boutique hotel with only 12 rooms right in the medina. This is Tunis's classiest hotel, if not its most expensive. ⓐ 64 Rue Sidi Ben Arous, Tunis ⓣ 71 563 022 ⓦ www.darelmedina.com ⓘ Booking ahead essential

Dar Hayet £££ One of the best-located hotels in Hammamet, the Dar Hayet Hotel has fantastic panoramic views across Hammamet Bay and is just a stroll from the resort centre. Comfortable, modern and charming accommodation. ⓐ Avenue El Aqaba, Hammamet ⓣ 72 283 399

Iberostar Jerba Beach Hotel £££ A very pleasant and efficiently run resort hotel on the beach in the Zone Touristique north of Midoun. The large rooms are clean and all have balconies. There's a large outdoor pool and gardens that open straight onto the beach. ⓐ Zone Touristique Sidi Mahrez, Djerba ⓣ 75 731 200

The Residence £££ Out on the beach not far from La Marsa, this luxurious hotel is a strange mix of business and leisure, but it probably has the best facilities of any hotel in the city, including a spa centre and indoor and outdoor pools. It takes about 20 mins to drive to the centre from here. ⓐ Les côtes de Carthage, La Marsa ⓣ 71 910 101 ⓦ www.theresidence.com

Preparing to go

GETTING THERE

The cheapest way to get to Tunisia is to book a package holiday with one of the leading tour operators that specialise in Tunisian holidays. You should also check the travel supplements of the weekend newspapers such as the *Sunday Telegraph* and the *Sunday Times*. Newspapers often carry adverts for inexpensive flights, as well as classified adverts for privately owned villas and apartments to rent in most popular holiday destinations. If your travelling times are flexible, and you can avoid the school holidays, you can find some very good-value last-minute deals using the leading holiday companies' websites.

By air

Most visitors use charter flights to get to Tunisia and these operate from nearly all of the UK's regional airports. Tunisair (020 7437 6236

⏶ *Tunisian harbour*

www.tunisair.com) and GB airways (0870 850 9850
 www.gbairways.com) run direct scheduled flights from London to
Tunisia. If you get an indirect flight (for example with Air France via
Paris), it can be less expensive but you have the inconvenience of having
to change planes. As a rule, the further in advance you buy a ticket the
cheaper it usually is. There are six international airports in Tunisia: Tunis,
Monastir, Djerba, Tozeur, Sfax and Tabarka.

Many people are aware that air travel emits CO_2, which contributes
to climate change. You may be interested in the possibility of lessening
the environmental impact of your flight through the charity Climate
Care, which offsets your CO_2 by funding environmental projects around
the world. Visit www.climatecare.org

By sea

There are ferries to Tunisia from Italy (Sicily, Sardinia, Naples and Genoa)
and France (Marseille).

TOURISM AUTHORITY

Further information about Tunisia can be obtained from the Tunisian
National Tourist Office 77A Wigmore Street, London W1U 1QF
 020 7224 5561 www.cometotunisia.co.uk. In Tunisia, you will find
Tourist Offices in every major town and tourist resort.

BEFORE YOU LEAVE

It is not necessary to have inoculations to travel to Tunisia, but you
should make sure that you and your family are up to date with the
basics, such as tetanus. It is a good idea to pack a small first-aid kit
containing plasters, antiseptic cream, travel-sickness pills, insect
repellent and/or bite-relief cream, antihistamine tablets, upset
stomach remedies and painkillers, sun lotion (especially of the
higher factor lotions if you have children with you), after-sun cream,
a hat and sunglasses.

If you are taking prescription medicines, ensure that you take enough
for the duration of your visit – you may find it impossible to obtain the

same medicines in Tunisia. It is also worth having a dental check-up before you go.

There are no health agreements in place with Tunisia so make sure that your travel insurance is valid and that it covers you for activities that you might want to try – such as scuba diving, watersports or even camel riding – and for emergency medical and dental treatment, including flights home if required.

ENTRY FORMALITIES

If you are a citizen of the UK, Republic of Ireland, the EU (with certain exceptions for Eastern European countries – check before departure), the USA or Canada, you do not need a visa to enter Tunisia (but always make sure you double check this before travel as conditions can change). Australian, New Zealand and South African citizens do need a visa. Other

⬤ *Some hotels in Tunisia offer extensive facilities for families*

important documents you will need are your tickets and your passport. Remember to check well in advance that your passport is up to date and has at least six months left to run. All children, including newborn babies, need their own passport now, unless they are already included on the passport of the person they are travelling with. It generally takes at least three weeks to process a passport renewal. This can be longer in the run-up to the summer months. For the latest information on how to renew your passport and the processing times contact the Passport Agency ☎ 0870 521 0410 ✉ info@passport.gov.uk ⊛ www.ukpa.gov.uk

If you are thinking of hiring a car while you are away, you will need to have your driving licence with you. If you want more than one driver for the car, the other drivers must have their licences too.

Tunisia does not have any sort of health care agreement with the UK. It is therefore strongly advised that you take out comprehensive medical insurance before you travel.

Duty free
You are allowed to bring the following amounts of goods duty free into the UK from outside the EU:
- Cigarettes or 100 cigarillos or 50 cigars or 250 g of tobacco.
- 2 litres of table wine.
- 1 litre of alcoholic beverages stronger than 22% or 2 litres of fortified or sparkling wine or other liqueurs.
- 60 ml of perfume and 250 ml of eau de toilette.
- Other goods including souvenirs up to the value of £145.

MONEY
The national currency is the Tunisian dinar (TD) and it is divided into 1,000 millimes (mills). A price of 1,500 millimes is usually quoted as 1.5 TD. It is a soft currency, which means that you cannot exchange or bring money from outside Tunisia or export it back out of the country with you. It is illegal to do so, so make sure you get rid of all your dinars before you leave Tunisia. Carry some cash with you when you arrive from your country, so that you can exchange it at the airport, because it can be

difficult to exchange traveller's cheques there. Most airports have ATMs where you can get dinars.

Exchanging money is fairly straightforward. In the tourist areas there are usually plenty of exchange bureaux and banks with ATMs. It may be worth doing a bit of research to get the best rate for your money or traveller's cheques.

Cash machines and credit cards

Most banks in the major cities and tourist resorts will have cash machines. In the main resorts you can usually find one that will accept your debit card, and you can take money directly out of your home account. In some towns you may have to use your credit card to take

● *Try to stay in the shade at midday*

money out at a cash machine, because not all of the local banks will recognise your debit card. Major credit cards are widely accepted in most hotels and shops, but some restaurants in non-tourist areas still do not accept them; you should therefore always carry some cash. If you are buying goods from stalls in souks and markets, make sure you have enough cash (euros, pounds sterling and US dollars are often accepted as well as dinars) as it is unlikely that you will be able to pay by card.

CLIMATE

Tunisia is a good place to visit (in terms of the weather) all year round. In the north, it gets cooler between late October and March, in the south (from Djerba southwards) the sun shines pretty much all year round and is a more bearable temperature in the winter months. The sun is very strong in Tunisia and the presence of a coastal breeze often means you can burn before you know it. Young children and people with fair skins can get badly sunburnt, so liberal use of a strong sunscreen and covering up, especially with a hat to cover the head, are to be recommended. Sunstroke can ruin your holiday, so do not try and get a good suntan in the first few days of your holiday. If you are planning to venture into the desert, remember that as well as extremely hot conditions during the day (all year round) it can also get very cold at night – make sure you bring warm clothing with you.

BAGGAGE ALLOWANCE

Baggage allowances vary according to the airline, destination and class of travel, but 20 kg (44 lb) per person is the norm for luggage that is carried in the hold (it usually tells you what the weight limit is on your ticket). You are also allowed one item of cabin baggage weighing no more than 5 kg (11 lb), and measuring 46 by 30 by 23 cm (18 by 12 by 9 in). In addition, you can usually carry your airport purchases, umbrella, coat, camera, and so on, as hand luggage. Large items – surfboards, golf clubs, collapsible wheelchairs and pushchairs – are usually charged as extras and it is a good idea to let the airline know in advance if you want to bring these.

During your stay

AIRPORTS

In all cases, your best best for getting out of the airports is to take a taxi. They are cheap and metered (make sure it is turned on when you get in!). Louage (shared taxis – see page 119) and bus services are also always available, but you may have to wait longer, although the fare will of course be cheaper than a taxi.

Tunis-Carthage International Airport (☎ 71 755 000) is about 10 km (6 miles) northeast of the city centre. A taxi to the centre will cost about TD 10. Car hire is available at the airport.

Djerba-Zarzis Airport (☎ 75 650 233) is 10 km (6 miles) from Houmt Souk. Car hire available.

Monastir H. Bourguiba Airport (☎ 73 460 300) is 10 km (6 miles) from the centre of Monastir. Care hire available.

Sfax-Thyna Airport (☎ 74 241 740) is 6km (4 miles) from Sfax. Car hire available.

Tozeur-Nefta Airport (☎ 76 450 342) is 4km (2½ miles) from town. Car hire available.

7 Novembre - Tabarka Airport (☎ 78 644 100) is 15 km (10 miles) from Tabarka. Car hire available.

COMMUNICATIONS

Telephones

International calls from hotel rooms are prohibitively expensive. It is less expensive to make phone calls from public phone boxes, taxiphone shops or telephones in post offices. You will need lots of change for call boxes. Some of the taxiphone shops (in most resort areas) let you pay for calls after you make them.

Most UK mobile phones will work in Tunisia, but check your rates before calling back to the UK from it. You can also buy SIM cards in Tunisia (about TD 5) to put in your own phone. But check with your provider in the UK to see whether this is possible before you go.

TELEPHONING TUNISIA
From abroad, dial the codes listed below followed by the 8-digit
local number
Australia & New Zealand 00 11 216
South Africa 090 216
UK & Ireland 00 216
US & Canada 011 216

PHONING ABROAD FROM TUNISIA
Dial the code listed below followed by the local number, minus
the initial 0
Australia 00 61
Canada 00 1
Ireland 00 353
New Zealand 00 64
South Africa 00 27
UK 00 44
US 00 1

Post offices

The postal system is fairly efficient, but you will likely be home before
any postcards that you send in the last week of your stay. You can usually
arrange *Poste Restante* facilities at the post offices (known as PTT). You
should be able to buy stamps (*timbres* in French) at most places that sell
postcards as well as in post offices.

CUSTOMS

Tunisia is the most liberal of the Muslim countries and there is
considerable freedom for women who live in cities and major tourist
resorts that have had many European visitors through the years.
However, although Tunisians seem in some ways to have adopted
Western values, they do not have the level of equality that women have

◔ *Letterbox on a house wall in Hammamet*

in Europe. In rural areas especially, the male domination of society is more obvious, religious values are more prevalent and women's roles in society are more rigidly defined. Many people in Muslim countries have a misconception about Western women and this is reinforced when they see women in skimpy clothing. This attitude is still present in some tourist resorts and you need to be aware of it. This does not mean you cannot strip off on a tourist beach (going topless is not advised, however); it just means that your holiday will be more hassle free if you wear what is appropriate at the right time. This means covering up your arms and legs when you leave the beach and especially if you are going to visit a rural area. It is also very important that both men and women cover up when going anywhere near a mosque; you may incur aggressive reactions from local people if you don't.

There are still men-only cafés in rural areas and even in some of the cities. Women will definitely attract unwelcome attention if they make the mistake of going into one of these either alone or in male company. The best way to prevent harassment is to avoid eye contact, to say a firm 'No' and to keep walking. It is a good idea for women to avoid areas where young males have gathered, but if they are cautious, especially at night, they will have an enjoyable holiday and keep the level of unwanted male attention to what you might reasonably expect to receive in any other Mediterranean country.

DRESS CODES

To avoid this unwanted attention, women should dress fairly conservatively, covering legs and at least the top parts of your arms. Wearing beachwear away from the beach and on the streets is likely to lead to problems. Likewise, men should not wander around without a shirt.

When going to visit mosques it is important not to wear shorts or revealing clothing or you will be refused entry.

ELECTRICITY

You will need a continental round-pin plug adaptor to use electric appliances you cannot live without. It is best to buy the adaptor at your departure airport, because they can be difficult to find in Tunisia. If you are considering buying electrical appliances to take home, always check that they will work in your country before you buy them (the voltage in Tunisia is 220 V, 50 Hz).

EMERGENCIES

If there is an emergency, dial 197 (police), 190 (ambulance) or 198 (fire) for the emergency services. You may need to find someone who speaks good French or Arabic to help you out if necessary.

The **British Embassy** is at ⓐ Rue du Lac Windermere, Les Berges du Lac, 1053 Tunis (ⓣ Switchboard: +216 71 108 700, out of working hours 98 319 128).

GETTING AROUND
Car hire and driving

This is an expensive option in Tunisia, but it does give you great freedom and independence if you want to head off and explore on your own. You need to be over 21 and have a valid driving licence. The least expensive option is to hire a car in your home country before you go. Alternatively, you can hire a car at the airport when you arrive or at the many car-hire offices in your resort. Although the local car-hire companies are usually a little cheaper, it is best to stick to the more reliable larger international car-hire firms, especially if you are taking a trip to the more remote areas of the country.

Driving is on the right-hand side of the road. You need to have confidence in your driving skills, particularly if you are doing some city driving, because the local drivers can be a little erratic and you can never quite be sure what will wander out onto the road – beast or fowl. The police (do not worry, they are very friendly!) will be at the entrance to every town and village and at roundabouts, so check your speed. The International Highway Code applies and speed limits are 50 km/h (31 mph) in towns, 90 km/h (56 mph) on trunk roads and 110 km/h (69 mph) on motorways. Roads are generally of good qualilty.

Train and metro

There is an efficient train service in Tunisia and this can be the best way to travel. The electric train (TGM) from Tunis runs to Carthage, Sidi Bou Said and the beach at La Marsa. There is also a local train service between Sousse and Sfax (via Monastir and Mahdia) and this makes travelling around this area comfortable and easy.

Taxis

In most cases, you will use a taxi to get around. It is the easiest way to get from your hotel to the airport and around the city centres. The most important thing to do is to take an official yellow taxi and to ensure that your driver uses the meter. At night the rate may be increased by 50 per cent and you can be charged extra for luggage.

Bus and louage

The bus service and louage (shared taxis) are the best way to cover large distances and go to places where the trains do not go.

HEALTH, SAFETY & CRIME
Health hazards

The best policy when trying to avoid stomach problems is to eat in good and clean cafés, restaurants and hotels. Spending a little more is worthwhile, rather than being ill for a day or two on your holiday. If you eat food prepared in very basic places that look unhygienic, you are more likely to get sick. This is especially important when you are eating shellfish, chicken and salads, because it is crucial to prepare these in a clean and sterile environment. If you do get a stomach bug and diarrhoea, you will need to rest. Drink lots of water and take rehydration preparations to replace the fluids you lose. If the symptoms persist for longer than 48 hours, ask your representative or your hotel reception staff to recommend a doctor because you will need to take medication.

Tap water is safe to drink in most places in Tunisia, but it does not taste very nice. It is best to drink bottled water, which is relatively inexpensive compared to UK prices and widely available. Tunisia is a much hotter and drier country than the UK and you must drink lots of water to keep hydrated. This is especially important if you participate in sporting activities, are walking in the middle of the day or take an excursion into the desert. It is also best that you do not drink too much alcohol in the middle of the day. Dehydration can make you seriously ill, so drink more water than you think you need.

The standard of medical treatment in Tunisia is very high, and many doctors have been trained in Europe, but if you do need hospitalisation it is important that you are taken to a private clinic and not to one of the state hospitals, which are of much lower standard. Most of the resort areas have special emergency ambulances on call to transport tourists who require hospital treatment. In the private clinics you are expected to pay upfront. It is important to have adequate medical insurance cover, so make sure you obtain travel insurance from a reputable source. For

⬤ *Eat in good, clean cafés and restaurants*

minor ailments you can go to a local GP. It is best to ask your
representative or the reception staff at your hotel to recommend one.

Pharmacies have a green and white sign. There is usually a duty
pharmacy open all night in the tourist resorts. Ask for details at your
hotel. There are a lot of over-the-counter medicines available in Tunisia
that would normally require a medical prescription at home, so you
can self-prescribe for some illnesses. You should not self-prescribe
antibiotics, however, because you cannot assume that the dose and
type of general antibiotic you are given is correct. If you are given an
ineffective antibiotic, your illness may get worse. If you are on prescribed
medication for a long-term illness or condition, make sure you take
adequate medication with you on holiday.

Beaches

On the main Tunisian beaches there are lifeguards and a flag safety system. Young children who are in the water should be closely monitored at all times. Swimming just after a big meal (wait an hour or more) or after drinking alcohol is dangerous and is not recommended.

Animals

Everyone is fascinated by camels, and this is a perfect chance to get up close to them. Although they have a reputation for being bad-tempered, most will be gentle and docile. Cats and dogs should be avoided because they tend to be wild and carry diseases. Do not pet or feed them, especially in areas where food is being consumed. There are some snakes and scorpions in Tunisia, but you are unlikely to meet them. In the desert, check your shoes (and the toilet!) for visitors, just in case.

Crime

Crime levels are very low in Tunisia and it is unusual to experience crime-related problems. Islam is very strict about crime and to commit a crime is considered shameful. On some tourist beaches, there are special tourist police to ensure that you have a safe and enjoyable holiday. Nevertheless, you should always be wary of pickpockets, especially in places where there are many distractions.

If you are the victim of a crime you will need to report it to the police. Remember to get them to provide you with a written report, since you will need it to claim money back from your insurer for things you have lost. This will take time (often several hours), but if you go along with someone who speaks French it might speed up the process. If you lose

BEACH SAFETY
Look out for the flag safety system:
- **White** – safe bathing and swimming
- **Black** – no swimming/dangerous winds or currents

your passport or if it is stolen you will need to go to the British Embassy in Tunis ⓐ Rue du Lac Windermere, Les Berges du Lac ⓣ 71 108 700 ⓛ 08.00–16.30 Mon–Thur, 08.00–13.00 Fri.

MEDIA

There is more choice when it comes to Tunisian television and radio than there used to be, with the opening up of the airwaves in 2005. English-language UK and American TV channels are available via satellite in most hotels. There are several Arabic and French-language newspapers but none published in English.

OPENING HOURS

Banks The official opening hours for banks are: Mon–Fri 08.00–11.30 (summer); 08.00–11.30 and 14.00–16.00 (winter). However, in tourist areas, they are likely to be open for longer hours. They are closed on Saturdays and Sundays everywhere. Exchange bureaux will probably open 08.00–20.00 daily in tourist resorts, but close for a time on Fridays.

Post offices Mon–Sat 08.00–13.00 (summer); Mon–Fri 08.00–12.00 and 14.00–18.00, Sat 08.00–12.00 (winter).

Restaurants Opening times of restaurants can be erratic and sometimes contradict the hours on the doors. Some restaurants do not open during the day, or even the evening, in the off-peak season. At other times, they may be open when you expect them to be closed. As a general rule, most open from 12.00 to 15.00 for lunch and then again in the evening from 17.30 to 22.00. Cafés and pizzerias tend to be open for longer (till about 24.00). If you want to eat in a specific popular restaurant, it is often best to book ahead. During the holy month of Ramadan, restaurants may shut down altogether or only open in the evenings, when there is a great party atmosphere.

Shops Opening times vary, but the better shops are usually open from 08.30 to 12.00 and 15.00 to 19.00. Markets are usually busiest in the morning, but in some tourist areas they go on all day or pick up again in the early evening. On Sundays and public holidays there may be nothing open at all.

RELIGION

Islam is the country's religion and it has an important impact on the way that people live. One of the distinct sounds of Tunisia is that of the *muezzin* (from '*mu'adhan*', meaning, 'call to prayer') chanting from the minaret towers of the mosques. This is one of the most significant roles in Islam since the faithful are called to prayer five times a day.

Tunisia is considered to be a liberal Muslim country and extremist Islamic groups are banned. There is a more relaxed attitude to religion than in the neighbouring countries of Algeria and Libya. Women have more freedom in how they dress and in Tunis the majority of the women wear Western clothing all of the time. You may even see some local men drinking alcohol and gambling, despite the fact that Islam prohibits these activities. On a Friday, when it is illegal for Tunisians to be sold beer, you may see locals drinking it. You may be asked to purchase some for them in a supermarket, but this is best avoided because it is a criminal offence for a retailer to sell alcohol to a Muslim on Fridays. You can, of course, buy beer for your own consumption.

For many Tunisians their religious belief is the most important thing in their life and you should respect this. In most cases you will only be allowed into the outer courtyard areas of the mosques, and only when it is not time for prayer. You cannot go into the prayer halls. The month of Ramadan is the most important time in the religious calendar. It usually falls sometime between late October and early November, depending on the lunar calendar. Restaurants and cafés are all likely to be shut during the day because the locals fast during daylight hours for the whole month, but in the evening the place buzzes with life.

TIME DIFFERENCE

Tunisia is one hour ahead of the UK in winter (Oct–March), but the same time in summer (March–Oct).

TIPPING

It really is up to you how much you tip hotel staff. The more expensive the hotel the more you will be expected to give. Most porter staff will expect a tip of 1 dinar at the very least. Taxi drivers do not normally expect tips (unless they give extraordinarily good service).

TOILETS

There is a scarcity of public toilets in Tunisia, and where they exist they are, like most public toilets in European countries, often not very clean and do not have paper. You are better off using lavatories in stations, restaurants, cafés and hotels.

TRAVELLERS WITH DISABILITIES

In general, the facilities in Tunisia are very poor for visitors with disabilities, particularly those who need to use a wheelchair. It is extremely difficult for wheelchair-bound travellers to get around in the city centres and impossible for them to get on and off most forms of public transport. The major resort hotels usually have good access and some facilities, but it is best to check with your travel agent before you leave. Access to restaurants and museums can be difficult.

Some general advice for the disabled traveller can be obtained from **Holiday Care Service** ⓐ 2 Old Bank Chambers, Horley, Surrey ❶ 0845 124 9971 Ⓦ www.holidaycare.org.uk

Those who have a good command of French can get some information about facilities for visitors with disabilities from the local Tunisian national organisation for the disabled (Institut de Promotion des Handicapés) in Tunis (❶ 71 520 588 Ⓦ www.iph.nat.tn).

A

accommodation 106–7
air travel 108–9, 113, 114
animals 121

B

baggage allowances 113
banks 122
beaches 10, 98
    safety 121
    see also individual locations
Berbers 8, 37, 78, 103
boat trips 99
Borj el Kebir 40
Bourguiba, Habib 9, 31, 32
British Embassy 117, 122
buses 114, 119

C

camel racing 103
camel rides 81, 86, 99, 100
carpets 70, 72
Carthage 8, 11, 54–7, 102
cash machines 112–13
casinos 19, 29
catacombs 25
Chbika 83, 84
children's entertainment 98–9
Chott El Jerid 84, 86
climate 113
crafts 22, 37–8, 40, 41, 66, 67–8
credit and debit cards 112–13
crime 121–2
customs, local 115–17

D

desert safaris 10, 82–8, 99, 100
disabilities, travellers with 124
Djerba 11, 36–42
Dougga 11, 62–5, 102
Douz 86–7
dress codes 116, 117
drinking water 119
driving 118
    car hire 111, 114, 118
    in the desert 82, 84

duty-free allowances 111

E

eating out 90–95, 99
    food hygiene 119
    opening hours 122
    see also individual locations
El Djem 11, 74–5
electricity 117
emergencies 117
entertainment and nightlife
    see individal locations

F

ferry services 109
festivals and events 75, 102–4
fishing 101
food and drink 90–95
football 100

G

golf 100
Guellala 38–40

H

Habib Bourguiba Mausoleum 31, 33
Hammamet 10, 14–19, 86, 102
hammams (Turkish baths) 17, 61
health 109–10, 111, 119–20
hookah pipes (*shisha*) 21, 42, 51, 53
Houmt Souk 40

I

inoculations 109
insurance 110, 111, 119
International Cultural Centre 15–16
Islam 8, 76, 104, 121, 123
    see also mosques

K

Kairouan 11, 70–3
kite and wind surfing 37, 101

L

La Ghriba synagogue 37–8
Lac de Tunis 45

land trains 99
language 94–5
louage (shared taxis) 114, 119

M

Mahdia 76–7
Malouf music 102–3
marinas 21, 32
Matmata 78–81
medical and dental treatment 110, 111, 119–20
medicines 109–110, 120
medinas 10–11, 17, 26, 31, 40, 46–7, 49, 72, 77
menu decoder 94–5
mirages 84
Monastir 10, 30–35
money 111–13
mosques 25, 32, 41, 46, 48, 70, 71, 72–3, 77, 116, 117, 123
museums 26–7, 34, 39–40, 46, 49, 55, 75

N

Nabeul 66–9
newspapers 122

O

Ong Ejjmal 87
opening hours 122

P

package holidays 108
passports and visas 110–111, 122
perfumes 50
pharmacies 120
police 117, 118, 121
Port el Kantaoui 20–23, 99
post offices 115, 122
pottery 37–8, 40, 41, 66, 67–8
Pupputt 17

R

Ramadan 104, 122, 123
Ribats 17, 27, 34, 35

Roman ruins 11, 17, 55–7, 62–5, 74–5, 99

S

Sahara Desert 8, 10, 82–8
sailing 101
shopping 96–7
  haggling 96–7
  opening hours 122
  see also individual locations
Sidi Bou Said 58–61
snorkelling and scuba diving 101
souks 11, 27, 49
Sousse 11, 24–9
sports and activities 100–101
sun safety 113

T

Tamaghza 84
Tamezret 81
taxis 114, 118, 119
telephones 114–15
television and radio 122
time differences 123
tipping 123–4
toilets 124
Toujane 81
tourist information 109
Tozeur 87–8
train and metro services 118
troglodyte homes 78, 79, 81
tuk tuks 99
Tunis 11, 44–53

W

weddings, Tunisian 104
women travellers 116–17

Y

yellow submarine trips 99

Z

zoo 50

ACKNOWLEDGEMENTS

We would like to thank all the photographers, picture libraries and organisations for the loan of the photographs reproduced in this book, to whom copyright in the photograph belongs:

Conor Caffrey (pages 9, 16, 18, 22, 23, 28, 33, 35, 38, 39, 41, 42, 45, 47, 48, 56, 58, 59, 60, 62, 64, 68, 71, 73, 74, 76, 79, 85, 87, 88, 89, 90, 93, 95, 96, 97, 101, 102, 108, 116, 120);

DREAMSTIME Jakezc (pages 10, 66), GM Valente (page 55), A Kaczmarek (pages 70, 83), M Novotny (page 98), P Sikora (page 105), E Zhulkov (page 110), Fornax (page 112)

Thomas Cook (pages 1, 5, 13, 26, 43, 80, 86, 103).

Wikimedia Commons (page 51)

I would like to thank the following people for their help in my research. Beccy Bichiou from Thomas Cook for her expert organisation, and Nabil, Hafedh and Said from the Tunisian Travel Service for the expert guidance and help.

Project editor and copy editor: Diane Teillol
Typesetter: Donna Pedley
Proofreader: Jan McCann
Indexer: Marie Lorimer

Send your thoughts to
books@thomascook.com

- Found a beach bar, peaceful stretch of sand or must-see sight that we don't feature?

- Like to tip us off about any information that needs a little updating?

- Want to tell us what you love about this handy little guidebook and more importantly how we can make it even handier?

Then here's your chance to tell all! Send us ideas, discoveries and recommendations today and then look out for your valuable input in the next edition of this title.

Email to the above address or write to:
HotSpots Series Editor, Thomas Cook Publishing, PO Box 227, Coningsby Road, Peterborough PE3 8SB, UK.